Rorty's Humanistic Pragmatism

Rorty's Humanistic Pragmatism

Philosophy Democratized

Konstantin Kolenda

University of South Florida Press / Tampa

The University of South Florida Press is a member of University Presses of Florida, the scholarly publishing agency of the State University System of Florida. Books are selected for publication by faculty editorial committees at each of Florida's nine public universities: Florida A&M University (Talla-hassee), Florida Atlantic University (Boca Raton), Florida International University (Miami), Florida State University (Tallahassee), University of Central Florida (Orlando), University of Florida (Gainesville), University of North Florida (Jacksonville), University of South Florida (Tampa), University of West Florida (Pensacola).

Orders for books published by all member presses should be addressed to University Presses of Florida, 15 NW 15th St., Gainesville, FL 32611.

Library of Congress Cataloging-in-Publication Data

Kolenda, Konstantin.
    Rorty's humanistic pragmatism : philosophy democratized / Konstantin Kolenda.
       p.   cm.
    Bibliography: p.
    Includes index
    ISBN 0-8130-0970-7
    1. Rorty, Richard. 2. Philosophy. 3. Methodology.
4. Pragmatism. 5. Humanism. 6. Postmodernism. I. Title.
    B945.R524K64 1990
191—dc20   89-49661
                                                          CIP

To Street and Edythe Fulton,
two edifying people

CONTENTS

ACKNOWLEDGMENTS

I wish to thank Rice University for its support of my research on this book. In 1987 I received a Mellon grant, relieving me of one semester's teaching. Allen Matusow, the dean of the humanities, supported my attendance at the Institute on Interpretation at the University of California in Santa Cruz, during the summer of 1988, when I had an opportunity to hear Richard Rorty's interchange with other participants on some topics covered in the book. Thanks are due to John Kekes, Olivia Orfield, Stephen Tyler, and William Wild, who read and commented on the manuscript in various stages of its development. I also wish to thank Teresa Saul of the University Presses of Florida for her superb copy-editing.

I am especially grateful to the subject of my book. In spite of many commitments, Rorty took the time to read my manuscript. While refraining from commenting on my interpretations of his views beyond suggesting that he saw them put in a right context, he limited himself to pointing out some factual and organizational infelicities. I therefore would not presume to claim that what I see in his work either meets or does not meet with his approval. But I must gratefully acknowledge his accessibility and openness. Unselfconsciously generous, he never failed to respond to my queries, and he made available to me his unpublished materials. For me, the manner of his response is an admirable example of what a philosophical conversation can be.

Rorty's Humanistic Pragmatism

Philosophy Democratized

The appearance of Richard Rorty's *Philosophy and the Mirror of Nature* in 1979 was a significant event on the American intellectual scene. That book raised the suspicion that academic philosophy in America, in spite of appearing vital and vigorous, was in fact in the doldrums of a dogmatic and docile slumber. To be aroused from such a slumber is not necessarily a welcome experience. But a competent gadfly is difficult to ignore and has to be dealt with, even if reluctantly. A reporter who examined our philosophical scene in 1987 concluded that "Richard Rorty makes philosophers squirm."[1] What caused this squirming?

Some of Rorty's readers see him as boldly proclaiming, or even gleefully advocating, "the end of philosophy." Although he emphatically rejects this interpretation, it is nevertheless partly supported by his desire to distinguish between Philosophy (uppercase) and philosophy (lowercase). In a long introduction to *Consequences of Pragmatism* (a series of essays written between 1972 and 1980 and supporting the conclusions defended in the other book), Rorty admitted that his inquiries "raised the question whether a culture could get along without Philosophy," although he would not predict what that post-Philosophical culture would look like beyond suggesting that people in such a culture "would not be those who knew a Secret, who had won through to the Truth, but simply people who were good at being human."

The claim that it is the philosopher's job to uncover the Truth about the Secret is the main target of Rorty's criticism. Leaning on other thinkers preceding him, he points to the confusions underlying attempts to discover the foundations of all knowledge or "Nature's Own Language." He claims that because the entire Western philosophical tradition from Plato to Kant was motivated by this inherently incoherent project, it is extremely difficult to avoid the conceptual traps laid by that tradition, which bestows on its practitioners a false sense of belonging to an authoritative elite entitled to lay down the parameters of an acceptable philosophical vocabulary.

So when Rorty questions the authority of contemporary successors to that tradition and suggests the possibility and desirability of making room for alternatives, he appears to be threatening the very being of the philosophical enterprise. When he encourages "hermeneutic" or "edifying" modes of philosophizing, he is seen by the philosophical establishment as abandoning the "time-honored" constraints on what constitutes good, respectable, and responsible philosophizing.

But the case can be made—and the objective of this book is to make it—that the shifts in the directions advocated by Rorty are in fact constructive and positive. As the title of this book, *Rorty's Humanistic Pragmatism: Philosophy Democratized,* suggests, the result of the shifts will be to expand the horizons of philosophy beyond the limits artificially imposed by restricting it to "officially" sanctioned channels and by the professionalization of the subject. When Rorty suggests that philosophers should regard themselves as "all-purpose intellectuals," he is not recommending that they cease being rigorous in their thinking. He merely reminds them that the activity of describing our experience should be open to the invention of new vocabularies and theories and as such should not be hindered by narrowly conceived barriers. If the dismantling of such barriers will allow other intellectuals—scholars in other fields and disciplines—to describe some of their inquiries as philosophical, this should not constitute a threat to those who talk about the same issues in the light of knowledge *they* acquired from studying the intellectual canon historically labeled philosophical.

One might envisage the post-Philosophical culture as a setting in which the label "philosophical" will not be bestowed only on those works by people with a Ph.D. degree in philosophy but on the works of any thinker whose purpose is to *be* philosophical about the subject matter in which he or she is competent. By the same token those persons brought up on analyses of texts traditionally labeled philosophical will not be seen as intruders when they apply insights gleaned from such analysis to literature, history, or theology. The fact that the views developed by such thinkers as Nietzsche, Heidegger, and Rorty himself have acted as invigorating stimuli in diverse fields of intellectual endeavor, combined with the recent willingness of practitioners in different disciplines to ignore their disciplinary boundaries and to carry on increasingly significant interdisciplinary work, testifies to the timeliness and the promise of the shifts advocated in Rorty's writings.

The main message of these writings is that we should take pragmatism seriously. By doing so, we will establish a closer connection between thought and life. To bring thought and life into a better balance, we should examine more carefully the notion of *coping*. Although that notion has a definite intellectual dimension—reflection, deliberation, taking thought—it also includes two other dimensions: action and hope. Knowledge, action, and hope are more closely intertwined than our philosophical tradition recognizes. That tradition has favored the first, epistemological, component. Immanuel Kant brought the other two into view when he formulated his three famous questions: What can I know? What ought I to do? What may I hope? In this book I propose to return to these questions in order to show how Rorty's views lead us toward better and more useful ways of dealing with experience.

Kant's question "What can I know?" need not direct our gaze toward the "conditions of all experience" and toward "the ultimate" in morality. Instead, it can put us in touch with truth as that which, in William James's informal formula, is good in the way of belief. Similarly, the question "What ought I to do?" can be discussed in ways that alert us to the full range of our practical experience and enable us to examine in concrete detail the ethical and political roles we may be called upon to play, without presupposing that there *must* be a connection between our private and our public lives. Finally,

Kant's question "What may I hope?" need not address itself to ultimate or transcendent possibilities but can be answered in terms of projects worthy of our attention in our mundane concerns and in our actual historical setting.

Pragmatism stresses the *holistic* character of experience, thus assuming that neither knowledge, nor action, nor hope can be fully explicated when taken by themselves. It sees human life as a concatenation of cognition, behavior, and expectation. It is skeptical of the possibility of keeping these three aspects of experience separated; they complement each other. But since our tradition has privileged knowledge, there are historical reasons for giving the dimensions of hope and action more attention. Rorty's pragmatism, by lifting to prominence the reactive and edifying dimensions of thought, recommends such a redirection. His questioning of the primacy of epistemology should be seen in the context of this larger project. Because Western philosophical tradition tended to favor heavily the epistemological dimension, those who cling to that tradition may find the proposed change of course disconcerting and even bewildering.

Readers of Rorty's recent book, *Contingency, Irony, and Solidarity,* published in 1989, may find it surprising that in his view topics of political justice are often treated more effectively in works of literature than in philosophical treatises. They may be reluctant to follow his recommendation not to aim at producing theories that would unify the private and the public aspects of human existence. This reluctance is rooted in the traditional assumption that self-creation and justice can be brought together at the level of philosophical theory. So when Rorty questions this assumption and instead points to imagination and utopian thinking as important vehicles of intellectual and moral progress, he is seen as advocating a new, unfamiliar kind of debate.

In the final chapter I examine some specific examples of this debate. Since Rorty's writings are now being translated into many other languages, this "conversation" will continue to be intense in academic circles all over the world. The debate concerns not only professional philosophy but also the uses of philosophical reflection in all forms of writing. We are reminded by Rorty that thought originating in any branch of intellectual activity *may* have practical consequences in the general cultural climate of opinion, but it is no less valuable when it produces no more than a constructive change in the thinker's or reader's self-image. This is the sense in which philosophy becomes democratized, allowing for intellectual growth in either the private or the public arena. I shall argue that, contrary to some initial fearful reactions, Rorty's humanistic pragmatism helps to enlarge, rather than restrict, the scope of philosophical reflection.

CHAPTER ONE

What Can I Know?

Pseudo-Objects of Knowledge

The philosophical workhorse of Western metaphysics is the distinction between appearance and reality. Introduced by the pre-Socratics and made especially prominent by Parmenides, it became the centerpiece of Plato's theory of knowledge. According to that theory, the world is but a highly imperfect copy of the World of Forms, eternally existing beyond time and space and only dimly accessible to properly prepared philosophical minds through a special activity Socrates called *anamnesis,* or recollection. Platonic realism postulated the possibility of encountering reality "wordlessly," by an act of intellectual seeing. Since the true nature of reality was encountered in the "mind's eye," it is not surprising that, inspired by Platonic realism, modern rationalistic philosophy could easily convert it into a form of idealism. As Rorty points out in *Philosophy and the Mirror of Nature,* the philosophical idea of the mind as the depository of knowledge was the invention of seventeenth-century philosophers. The ghostlike operations of consciousness are supposed to put us in *direct* touch with reality, seen mythically by Plato as the World of Forms and later demoted by Kant to the transcendent and mysterious thing-in-itself.[1] Even the empiricists—Locke, Berkeley, and Hume—provided a link between the rationalists and Kant by embracing the theory that knowledge consists of inspecting ideas imprinted on the mind. Locke viewed ideas as copies or representations of realities to which they are said to correspond, although he was unsure how to describe this alleged correspondence. According

1

to Rorty, "Locke was balancing awkwardly between knowledge-as-identity-with-object and knowledge-as-true-judgment-about-object."[2] Like many of his philosophical successors, Locke failed to recognize that the ability to respond to stimuli "is a causal condition for knowledge but not a *ground* for knowledge."[3]

To his credit, Locke was uneasy about his theory of knowledge as representation and struggled to overcome its difficulties by various unconvincing devices, including, on the one hand, the stipulation of direct, "sensitive" knowledge and, on the other, embracing rationalist and theological accounts of morality. Hume similarly tried to avoid the pitfalls of idealism with his distinction between ideas and impressions, but ultimately he resigned himself to skepticism. The boldest of the three empiricists, George Berkeley, declared that the function played in Plato's theory of Forms and later lodged by Kant in the thing-in-itself was to be assigned to the only ultimate reality—God. When we think correctly we are only copying God's thoughts, concluded Berkeley.

Some of Berkeley's reasoning was difficult to refute, even though, as Hume confessed, it produced no conviction. If the knowledge we have can be only of ideas, and if nothing can be like an idea except another idea, then the correspondence theory of truth is a sham. That theory postulates the existence of an inaccessible isomorphism between language and nonlinguistic reality. While Berkeley followed out the logical consequences of the Cartesian-Lockean picture of the mind, he nevertheless put his finger on a difficulty that has kept resurfacing in modern philosophizing, eventually taking the form of an attack on the "myth of the given." "The given" is supposed to be the ultimate referent of ideas or thoughts, without itself being in the nature of an idea or a thought capturable in language. But if so, how can we think it, make sense of it?

Kant's resort to some specific formal features of the mind that supposedly convert into knowledge the raw material of the given—the so-called manifold of sensation—was only half successful, according to Rorty. It did constitute an "advance in the direction of a propositional rather than a perceptual view of knowledge," but it still blurred the distinction between justification and causal explanation, because "it was contained within the framework of causal metaphors—'constitution,' 'making,' 'shaping,' 'synthesizing,' and the like."[4]

There is no direct access to any kind of given; it always must be articulated in some vocabulary. Causal explanation is no substitute for justification. The very idea of giving sense to anything without language is self-stultifying, because sense-making and language are coextensive. Rorty makes this point when he observes that "the *only* force of saying that texts do not refer to nontexts is just the old pragmatist chestnut that any specification of a referent is going to be in some vocabulary."[5] In order to describe any reality, the describer needs words or signs that are already meaningful, that is, have intelligible, shareable use. The so-called linguistic turn in philosophy, brought about by the work of Wittgenstein, Ryle, and Austin, was anticipated by earlier thinkers, including the American philosopher C. S. Peirce. Peirce attacked the Cartesian intuitions and the Kantian thing-in-itself by introducing his theory of signs, according to which the reference of a sign is always to another sign. Neither direct intuiting, seeing in the mind's eye something unthinkable, nor the apprehension of the thing-in-itself makes sense, he argued. If we take signs to be equivalent to some form of language, there is no escape from the maze of words.[6]

Peirce's early attack on the given received later support in the detailed work of Quine and Sellars.[7] All these critics of the Platonic tradition convinced Rorty that it is a mistake to regard the truth of propositions as grounded in that to which propositions refer. The mistake lies in giving the notion of truth two very different employments. It is supposed to characterize (1) the property of *propositions* (statements, judgments) and (2) the property of the *relations* that propositions have to something nonpropositional or nonlinguistic (reality, nature, facts). We ought to question the meaning of the second employment. By running together these two employments the Platonic tradition covered up the incoherence of its philosophical distinction between appearance and reality.[8] When examined more closely, that juxtaposition reveals an attempt to reconcile two irreconcilables. Nothing merely "given" *justifies* us in accepting a proposition or a belief.

While acknowledging the stubbornness of sensation (taken note of by Peirce in his category of Secondness), Rorty warns against treating it as signaling a transcendent metaphysical reality. Such a postulation gets us nowhere, because it fails both as an explanation and as justification. We get no explanation when we are asked to stop

3

with something given, directly intuited. In that regard, Rorty accepts the misgivings offered by Berkeley and Peirce. The transcendental move wishes to terminate thought in nonthought. But this is an impossible, self-contradictory wish. The validity of the *thought* is to be vouched for or guaranteed by something that *transcends* thought.

Taking a cue from Donald Davidson, Rorty recommends that we cease speaking of the supposed "content" to which our "schemes" somehow correspond. To talk about our conceptual scheme is to refer "to what we believe now—the collection of views which make our present-day culture."[9] If we acknowledge the temporary character of such schemes, the scheme-content distinction becomes problematic. That distinction encourages the blurring of the difference between truth claims as generated *within* language use and alleged truth claims of the way these "internal" truth claims hook up with something outside them. Wittgenstein also was struck by the highly problematic nature of that latter relationship when at the end of the *Tractatus* he declared that all propositions of that ingenious work are nonsensical. They are nonsensical because they are trying to say the unsayable. In his later work, Wittgenstein warned about language idling or going on holiday. Rorty endorses this line of argument and thinks that, like Wittgenstein, he is merely helping to destroy houses of cards. He invites us to shift our attention to the *substance* of being in the world, namely our concrete activities of coping manifested in successful uses of language. These uses are highly variegated and grow organically within specific cultures and multiple domains of human interest.

Real Objects of Knowledge

The appearance-reality distinction need not be interpreted as Plato interpreted it. Understood as lacking such pretensions, it does nothing more dramatic than help us move from false propositions to true propositions, from mistaken judgments to veridical claims. As Rorty says, "The distinction between reality and appearance seems merely the distinction between getting things right and getting things wrong."[10] Among the philosophers who helped Rorty escape the bewitching attraction of Platonic metaphors was Ludwig Wittgenstein. His simple but telling account of how we acquire the mastery of color words, for example, points to a different way of describing our contact with reality. According to Wittgenstein, our knowledge of colors is manifested in the behavior we exhibit in the presence of colors. Some of the behavior is linguistic, that is, identifying colors, classifying them, being able to pick out and to point correctly to colored shapes, etc. Whether we *really* see colors is shown in successful performances of such activities, accompanied by appropriate words. This is why Wittgenstein says quite seriously that a proper answer to the question "How do you know that this is red?" would be "I have learned English."[11] The language gives us a most reliable access to reality, because reliability and reality are logically connected. When we say that reality is that which can be relied upon, we are acknowledging the secure functioning of our language. What the real world *is* is revealed to us in the successful use of language. Seeing is believing, and beliefs are expressed in language.

Rorty sees a close connection between Peirce's theory of signs and Wittgenstein's claim that we can never escape the maze of language.[12] He reaffirms the Wittgensteinian point when he says that "the world is out there, but descriptions of the world are not—the world does not speak. Only we do."[13] This point is raised by Rorty against every attempt to see the connection of a linguistic expression or a thought to something nonlinguistic in terms of the alleged truth relationship. Proponents of such views accept them because they believe that they must answer the skeptic who demands a foundation or a justification of a knowledge claim. But, as not only Berkeley and Peirce but also Quine and Sellars made abundantly clear, we cannot get hold of that to which a sentence or a thought or a concept refers except by means of another linguistic term. There is no other way in which thought hooks up with reality. As Rorty puts it, "To say that truth is not out there is simply to say that where there are no sentences there is no truth, that sentences are elements of human languages, and that human languages are human creations."[14]

The conclusion to be drawn, according to Rorty, is that what lies "on the other side" of language or thought does not make any epistemological contribution to knowledge. It does not constitute a "world" and indeed it *constitutes* nothing. As such it is irrelevant and of no epistemological interest. By ceasing to talk about it we lose nothing at all. Indeed, as Rorty puts it in the title of one of his articles, it is "The World Well Lost." He sums up this argument as follows:

> I want to claim that 'the world' is either the purely vacuous nothing or the ineffable cause of sense and goal of intellect, or else a name for the objects that inquiry at the moment is leaving alone: those planks in the boat which are at the moment not being moved about. It seems to me that epistemology since Kant has shuffled between these two meanings of the term 'world,' just as moral philosophy since Plato has shuffled back and forth between 'the Good' as a name for an ineffable touchstone of inquiry which might lead to the rejection of *all* our present moral views, and as a name for the ideally coherent synthesis of as many of those views as possible. This equivocation seems to me essential to the position of those philosophers who see 'realism' or 'the correspondence theory of truth' as controversial or exciting theses.[15]

To find "the world" (as thus understood) of no philosophical interest is not to be left with mere language. As J. L. Austin insisted, language is never *mere*. Linguistic practices are substantive phenomena of our lives and supply us with veridical beliefs. According to Peirce, to hold a belief is to hold it to be true, that is, to be prepared to act on it, to use it for prediction and control. Thus, there is a commonsensical and uncontroversial use of the term "world" that is equivalent to the sum total of warranted beliefs making up our experience. One might say that our beliefs actually *present* the world to us in their multifarious and largely coherent connections; they are not just *about* the world. The web of beliefs *gives* us the world. True sentences are not merely intimating or hinting at something beyond them but *show* us reality as it makes up our experience. They give not only the *form* of that reality but also its *substance*.[16]

We may be less tempted to talk about language-transcending realities if instead of saying that language helps us cope with the world we simply say that language helps us cope. "Coping" already includes the acknowledgment of objective realities that language takes into account in being used. In Wittgenstein's view, as in Austin's, language is never "mere"; in knowing the word "tree," for example, we know what trees and forests are, and in knowing color words we can describe a rainbow. There is no denying that what we understand by reality is the large body of normal and familiar facts acknowledged in noncontroversial and incontrovertible statements. Correspondingly, what we mean by rationality in part consists in reacting appropriately to such statements, that is, treating them as providing stable and veridical information about the world. Meaningful statements have their truth-conditions. If someone doubts whether, say, this is a hand, then it is clear that he or she does not know the meaning of the word "hand." [17] In Rorty's view, "rationality" is a name "for a suitable balance between the respect for the opinions of one's fellows and respect for the stubbornness of sensation." [18]

That there is such a thing as evidence for beliefs would be fatuous to deny. Natural science is *natural* precisely because it is possible to single out a large body of facts and regularities that remain constant and stable enough to allow us to formulate theories about them. Nevertheless, such facts and regularities are not independent of theories for the simple reason that the *descriptions* of those facts and regularities are language-dependent. They must be supported by "the opinions of one's fellows," that is, fellow speakers of a linguistic community. In *Philosophy and the Mirror of Nature* Rorty was inclined to side with the position taken by Dewey and Wittgenstein, which he labeled "epistemological behaviorism" or "pragmatism" and which explains rationality and epistemic authority by reference to what society lets us say, rather than explaining the latter by the former. [19] To take this position is to conclude that "philosophy will have no more to offer than common sense (supplemented by biology, history, etc.) about knowledge and truth." [20]

A linguistic community may acquire a high degree of sophistication, refinement, and complexity—as is the case in modern science. The greater the sophistication, the narrower the community, because the initiation into that community requires special and extended training. At the frontiers of science it seems literally true, says Rorty, that what is accepted as scientifically sound depends on what our fellows let us get away with. Their authority is partially derived from what shows up on their screens and on their measuring apparatuses. They maintain that authority as long as they can back it up with the unquestioned "stubbornness of sensation," acknowledged in the normal responses of human senses.

How Knowledge Grows

The impressive fact about modern science is its incredible growth. The fact of change and growth gives rise both to skeptical thoughts and to attempts to overcome them by constructing overarching or underlying universal schemes somehow guaranteed by "the nature of things." Seeing that beliefs accepted in one epoch are replaced by often incompatible beliefs, that an established vocabulary gives way to a seemingly incommensurable successor vocabulary, insults our Parmenidean urge to reach after the Truth divinely valid for all times and all contexts. Perceiving the illegitimacy and the chimerical nature of the Parmenidean urge, Rorty recommends that we switch our attention to the specific truth claims generated in various fields of human activities and devote ourselves to the task of articulating them more fully and perspicuously, keeping in mind the particular purposes and objectives which are served or frustrated by our ways of talking. A significant part of that attention will be understandably directed at points where we perceive problems, confusions, and inconsistencies, that is, at situations in which the prevalent vocabulary is under strain and where a new vocabulary seems desirable. That vocabulary is likely to conflict at least in part with the previous one. Rorty sees the avant-garde aspect of any inquiry as the most interesting phase of intellectual life.

The growth of knowledge does not consist in getting our descriptions and theories closer to an independently existing reality. To make such claims, there would have to be some language-neutral access to that reality. There is no such access; every account must be in *some* language, a language that articulates both the data and the theories. "The same" phenomena, the celestial bodies, or pieces of matter on earth are seen differently because the new theories and vocabularies are generated to describe their so far unattended features, for instance, their molecular or atomic structures. The new truths of science are new not because nature has changed but because the accounts and theories have. It is this proliferation of explanatory frameworks, each illuminating the so far unexplored corners of nature, that gives rise to the charge of relativism. Those who raise it point to the discovery that paradigm changes even in science are often arbitrary inventions, creatively concocted to deal with intractable phenomena, that is, phenomena that could not be explained by previously accepted theories.

The relativism charge is harmless, however, as long as it is admitted that *all* phenomena are relative to the language in which they are described. And if it is the case that a change in language allows *better* descriptions, descriptions that help us predict and control more phenomena or aspects of phenomena so far baffling or unnoticed, then the vocabularies that help bring this change about are to be welcomed as truth-revealing. These truths will, of course, be new, and in some cases they can be so successful as to overshadow or set aside the truth-revealingness of previous theories, making them to that extent false. This was the fate of the Newtonian theory when corrected by Einstein's theory. A similar transformation seems to be occurring in biology as the theory of evolution is reformulated to take into account new discoveries about the behavior of living cells, for instance, the role of DNA.

Rorty is not denying that scientific or commonsense-factual beliefs have grounds. Not all beliefs are warranted, only those that are supported by facts in the straightforward and unmysterious sense of "fact" as the state of affairs unquestioned by participants in a given linguistic community. Scientists in the laboratory also constitute a linguistic community. They formulate statements that are tested both against the requirement of a theory and the observations inspectable and confirmable by competent practitioners of a given inquiry. Just which observations are deemed relevant and revealing emerges in the course of dealing with phenomena of interest to the investigators. These phenomena are of interest because, while in part subject to prediction and control, in other respects they are not understood; that is, they are *not* subject to prediction and control, or they fail to cohere with other established truths. The line between those that are not understood and those that are keeps shifting, and the change is made to enlarge knowledge. The change is not arbitrary but is determined by what is testable and falsifiable. What is really the case is the product of the agreement that emerges in the community of investigators.

This view of scientific objectivity in no way questions the advance of knowledge as it emerges from experimentation, from the introduction of new techniques and paradigms, and from surprising or unexpected discoveries. It is to be expected, however, that at the edges of any inquiry there will be a greater need to *introduce* new vocabularies and new theories for the simple reason that the existing ones are not adequate to deal with the complexity manifested by the phenomena in question. The introduction of new theories and new terms brings about a further penetration into the so far unknown aspects of phenomena. We could not make sense of these aspects; they were not even candidates for knowability until, by introducing new terms, ways were found to put them into conceptual/cognitive relationships to aspects already understood. Objectivity of facts is a function of understanding them. Scientists can tell us what is objectively the case when they have understood the state of affairs in question. They stop short of asserting that something is objectively the case when they are puzzled or uncertain, when the phenomena in question appear baffling, allowing of no adequate linguistic formulation. Utilizing Quine's metaphor, Rorty suggests that those beliefs that can be successfully woven into the web of already accepted ones deserve to be labeled as objectively true.

Descriptions of the world (in a straightforward, nonphilosophical sense) can be either commonsensical or scientific. The latter, like the former, indicate unforced agreement by the members of a given linguistic community. In the case of scientific knowledge, especially that of a specialized sort, the respective communities vary in size and in some instances may constitute a rather small number of experts. The truth of statements believed is not the function of agreement alone but also of vocabulary and procedures that make up the confirmed and accepted mechanisms of inquiry and justification. When unforced agreement is sufficiently widespread, the beliefs acquire the status of what Thomas Kuhn dubbed "normal science," as contrasted with situations characterized by experimental, innovative, or "revolutionary" vocabularies and procedures. Revolutionary changes by definition do not appeal to already established concepts and criteria. In contrast, familiar phenomena *are* familiar because no member of a linguistic community has any difficulty identifying paradigms of an appropriate language and the criteria of truth covering these phenomena. Willful departures from such established uses are understandably called irrational because they in fact fail to produce the success, the prediction, and the control normally enjoyed by the rest of the linguistic community. The distinction between rationality and irrationality is properly at home in "normal science" where criteria for establishing warranted beliefs are available. But when important shifts in vocabulary occur, such criteria have not yet been developed, and hence the notion of rationality does not obtain.[21]

The rational/irrational distinction is problematic at the edges of any given area of knowledge, where informed consensus is lacking. To introduce a new word or to extend a familiar concept in an unfamiliar way is to go outside the area of unforced agreement and to invite the members of the linguistic community to think differently about a segment of reality. Whether the new or modified concept or theory will catch on is an open question. If other members of the community follow the innovator and begin to use the concept in the suggested way, the linguistic behavior of that community will change. Following Davidson's account of metaphors, Rorty points out that the adoption of new words is not consequent upon the discovery of new antecedent meanings but consists in the creation of further meanings. The creator of a metaphor does not have a *reason* for his or her way of talking, for the presence of such a reason would make it possible to subsume the metaphor under an already existing criterion. Nevertheless, it may be possible to find a *cause* behind the introduction of the metaphor in question. If it catches on and becomes understood and used in the way suggested by its creator, the metaphor may in time become "dead," that is, may be included among other literal meanings of linguistic expressions.[22]

Rorty does not regret the loss of "the world" understood as a set of preexisting meanings somehow lighted upon or discovered by the power of thought, because he would like to leave room for discoveries and extensions of knowledge due to creative contributions made by new metaphors and new theories. The world as a concatenation of phenomena brought to expression in the use of language is not found but made. But what language manages to take hold of is not ephemeral; to the extent that a linguistic use is suc-

11

cessful, it gives objectivity and reality to experience. The phenomena with which we cope and which are reflected in our behavior are in that sense *well* made—we find our way in the world and understand our surroundings.

Like other human creations, language is a product of time and chance.[23] We are not tempted to think of the innumerable languages that have come into being in the course of human history as copying some preexistent structures. All languages are contingent in the sense that the connection between sounds or signs that language users make and what those uses accomplish is invented, "nonnatural." It is non-natural in the sense that a sound used to refer to a body of water, for example, is arbitrary; it so happens that *this* sound and not another has acquired currency in this particular role. It could have been different, and as a matter of fact it *is* different in another linguistic community, even though it performs the identical job of referring to a body of water.

Once a word, a phrase, or a sentence acquires common currency or semantic conventional meaning, we sensibly forget that its origin was arbitrary. We certainly don't call its *use* arbitrary for the simple reason that by becoming conventional it *ceases* being arbitrary; it is now tied to a segment of a form of life. Having arisen in the context of coping with some phenomena, it can be correctly invoked in the presence of these phenomena. To say that language as a whole is "something which can be adequate or inadequate to the world or to the self"[24] is to utter an empty remark because for something to *be* a bit of language is to display a criterion of adequacy in a bit of behavior or coping. Whoever understands a locution and acts in the way it specifies shows in part what adequacy *is*.

We should be wary of such questions as: What kind of instrument is language? How does it work? Or even more globally, What *is* language? Seeing through the misleading character of such questions, Davidson has concluded that "there is no such thing as a language, not if a language is anything like what many philosophers and linguists have supposed."[25] Bits of language can represent, communicate, or express, but one should not conclude from this that language is a *medium* of representation, communication, or expression. As Rorty, following Davidson, suggests, the customary purposes of language use can be frustrated by "mumbles, stumbles, malapropisms, metaphors, tics, seizures, psychotic symptoms, egregious stupidity, strokes of genius and the like."[26] Whether such "infelicities" occur is a contingent matter. Normally, we do not expect them to happen, but when they do, we have ways of recognizing them for what they are and how to compensate for them.

Of course, we are not alive to surprising contingencies of language when things go smoothly, when the words and sentences we hear or speak are familiar and evoke normal, habitual responses. But even in such contexts we need to remain alert as to the point or drift of a narrative or an argument; usually we do not know ahead of time where it will lead or what it will disclose or accomplish. If we did, we would not need language. To make ourselves understood, we resort to comparisons, analogies, and metaphors, verbally pointing to connections that will produce understanding in our interlocutor's mind. Some metaphors may turn out to be more fruitful than their original utterers could foresee. When made use of by other speakers, a metaphor will introduce a new bit of vocabulary into a language, thus contributing to its growth or change.

Following Davidson, Rorty views metaphor not as disclosing antecedently existing meanings but as causing us to shift attention to some unsuspected connection between the already existing vocabulary and the phenomena it was intended to cover. A live metaphor is an instance of blindly or experimentally hitting on a locution that causes us to put familiar language to a new use. Pragmatically speaking, we hit upon a tool that *happens* to work better than previous tools. Since all language is arbitrary in the sense that its original tokens caused meanings (as meaningful behavior) to arise, Rorty thinks it plausible to regard the history of language as the history of metaphor.[27] The intellectual history of humanity, or, in the old vocabulary, the development of mind, may be seen as the accumulation of metaphors which in time gain sufficient currency to become literal meanings. "Old metaphors are constantly dying off into literalness, and then serving as a platform and foil for new metaphors."[28]

Our access to reality, then, is not to be understood as comparing bits of language to some supposed language-independent facts. We get at the facts of the case by coming up with descriptions that result in better prediction and control. We get a grasp of facts not by penetrating more deeply into phenomena themselves but by inventing new ways of describing them (not geology but geography). Whether our grasp of facts or reality is better or not depends on how our descriptions connect with already successful descriptions. As Rorty suggests, "The world does not provide us with any criterion of choice between alternative metaphors, . . . we can only compare languages or metaphors with one another, not with something beyond language called 'fact.'"[29]

How Self-Knowledge Is Acquired

As we need not penetrate Nature's Own Language to have objective knowledge about natural phenomena, so we need not assume that in order to come up with veridical descriptions of ourselves and of other human beings we must begin with a search for Essential Human Nature. Rorty thinks that we should "set aside the idea that both the self and reality have intrinsic natures, natures which are out there waiting to be known."[30] We find *ourselves* to be objective and intelligible entities inasmuch as we say true things about our beliefs, desires, interests, hopes, and wishes. There is a large, unproblematic, thoroughly transparent area in the behavior of human beings, as each of us habitually produces true first-person statements and true descriptions of the behavior and experiences of others. Much of what we say about ourselves and about others is not hidden either from the speakers or from their hearers.[31]

As our knowledge of the world changes in light of the contingent contributions of our changing language, so does our conception of ourselves. Since our beliefs and desires are directed toward phenomena we try to predict and control, we come to know our traits, dispositions, tendencies, possibilities, and limits as we follow the career and vicissitudes of our attempts to cope. Certainly, in time we begin to see that there are continuities, regularities, habits, and hang-ups in our responses and behavior. In other words, we come to develop an individual character as it emerges in the process of experience. But just as it is an error to think of the world as manifesting certain persistent structures prior to and independent of our attempts to describe them, so it is an error to see ourselves as manifesting an antecedent human nature which our self-knowledge supposedly discovers.

Rorty credits Freud with having shown convincingly that self-creation is characteristic of human beings. In this regard, Freud followed in the footsteps of Nietzsche, who thought of man as a "peculiar sort of dying animal who, by describing himself in his own terms, had created himself."[32] Rather than thinking of the human self as a well-ordered system of faculties, we should think of it as a tissue of contingent relations.

If self-creation is conversion of contingencies into idiosyncratic selves, then there cannot be such a thing as a paradigm human being. The attempts to subordinate human reality to some necessary pattern, biologically, theologically, or morally prestructured, fly in the face of facts. To speak of something being "truly human" is to return to the citadel of necessity, in which, in Kantian fashion, we confront "the same imperatives, the same unconditional claims."[33] To live in such a citadel is to have no room for "programming our lives or our poems." Freud's important contribution was to alert us to the role that unconscious fantasy plays in our attempts at self-programming. "For Freud, nobody is dull through and through, for there is no such thing as a dull unconscious."[34] No person's contingencies are "processed" in the same way because, in addition to conscious, deliberate weighing and judging, there are also the unpredictable and unforeseeable reactions of the unconscious, the submerged, or the instinctive aspects of human organisms.

Special self-creating individuals are the strong poets who are not content with "shoving about already-coined pieces," that is, following in the ready-made tracks of their predecessors. They each go their own way, creating new metaphors and new descriptions, and thus, like Nietzsche, convert their lives into literary creations.[35] What is special about such strong individuals is that they are capable of discerning the special influences that helped them become the persons they are. They are good at acknowledging and appropriating contingency. What they become is in part a matter of luck and in part a witness to their alertness in converting contingencies into significant facts. Freud showed us, claims Rorty, that "only if we catch hold of crucial idiosyncratic contingencies in our past shall we be able to make something worthwhile of ourselves, to create present selves whom we can respect."[36]

There is no predicting which flights of fancy, hunches, and

metaphors will move beyond personal and idiosyncratic contexts and will spill over onto the public stage. In Rorty's view, "poetic, artistic, philosophical, scientific, or political progress results from the accidental coincidence of a private obsession with a public need."[37] Eccentricity is not always perversity; it is a de-centering that blindly strikes out in a new direction or breaks new, fertile ground. Whether the new road will be traveled or whether the fertile soil will sprout seeds is also a contingent matter, and in that regard the innovator's success depends on the alertness, cooperation, preparation, or goodwill of the successors. T. S. Eliot claimed that whether a poet is understood depends on the readers' collaboration, and Dewey suggested that the beholder of any work of art "must *create* his own experience." In an esthetic perception, "we must summon energy and pitch it at a responsive key in order to *take* in."[38]

When likened to a work of art, no human life is ever finished in its implications, because of its open-ended dependence on the future. This fact can understandably trigger a good deal of anxiety about the meaning of one's life. Rorty quotes a phrase from Nabokov's *Pale Fire:* "Man's life as commentary to abstruse unfinished poem."[39] The recovery of the web of one's beliefs, desires, designs, and hopes can never be fully completed, *pace* Nietzsche's hope for the Overman—but, while leaving many strands loose and uninterpreted, the person's at least marginal imprint cannot be erased.

How Communities Come into Being

The open-ended reality of human selves also affects their relations to others. Although not governed by a common nature, they can create communities by establishing consonance and harmony with some others. The kinds of groupings that emerge— tribes, nations, economic classes, cultural organizations—are contingent on the success of individuals in establishing ties to one another that persist over time, effecting the emergence of traditions. The great variety of cultures and institutions that define themselves around a common set of practices and goals should discourage speculations about the uniformity and unity of human nature. What distinguishes *homo sapiens* from other species is that its biological uniformity does not determine its cultural forms. Such forms are of course made possible by certain common physical features, but the character of those forms cannot be deduced from these features or from any other facts.

When human communities articulate and disseminate their particular values, they address only those who by virtue of the contingency of given circumstances are susceptible to persuasion concerning the desirability of these values. Seeing themselves as falling under certain cultural descriptions—as individuals and as members of a community—language users are not likely to look upon these descriptions as expressing preestablished facts but rather as constituting optional and desirable forms of life. Of course, there may be a strong temptation, especially in early, primitive stages, to view these forms of life as the only right ones, perhaps even as a species of natural facts. In such social contexts outsiders are seen as barbarians, amenable not to persuasion but only to conquest, to forcible conversion. But in time such a restricted reading of human possibilities is likely to be recognized as arbitrary, in the sense of not being tied to some absolutely constraining facts, and thus not an inevitable expression of uniform human nature.

How can communities justify their beliefs, traditions, and values? When philosophical about it, they may attempt, as Hegel recommended, to "grasp their time in thought." The "foundation" for such a justification is not something supposedly shared by all humanity but specific values with which the members of the community are prepared to identify. They see their past and their tradition as made possible by these values. Rorty notes that cultural justification and criticism are inevitably circular; they cannot be undertaken from an impartial standpoint. We criticize one feature of our culture by citing another, or we compare "our culture invidiously with others by reference to our own standards."[40] If by justification is meant a reference to some ahistorical, universalist foundation, cultural norms and practices cannot be justified, according to Rorty. Rather, he thinks that "to offer a redescription of our current institutions and practices is not to offer a defense of them against their enemies; it is more like refurnishing a house than like propping it up or placing barricades around it."[41]

What can a member of a social community say in response to the question "How do you *know* that the values of your commu-

17

nity deserve your allegiance?" To identify with such values is to see them as preferable, for a variety of specifiable reasons, to alternative values embraced by other communities. Thus, for example, one can point to the greater fairness and advantages of a political system that allows for free elections over a system in which people are not free to choose the persons who will lead them. Besides horizontal comparisons with other coexisting forms of life, it is also possible to contrast the present state of affairs with its historical predecessors. Indeed, there is no other way of evaluating those predecessors except in terms of what one now believes to be preferable. No evaluation is possible from a neutral position, because to evaluate *is* to apply some standards of what is worth having. The only place from which one can begin is that place which one is occupying. This starting point, however, is not arbitrary, because what one values has won out over its potential rivals, contemporary or historical, and can be supported by reasons.

The process by which one arrives at a commitment to the values one holds is multidimensional, and it does not involve deduction from some preexistent grid. The kind of apologetics to which people resort when asked why they have the moral or political beliefs they actually profess is more like a narrative than an algorithm. Rorty suggests that allegiance to social institutions must be seen as no more arbitrary "than choice of friends or heroes."[42] An explanation of why a certain scientist, philosopher, or poet is important, or why a given historical or contemporary event deserves attention, will draw on the allegiances, the commitments, and the projects of the explainer. Apart from such concrete, historically contingent evaluations of what is worth upholding or defending, such explanations are either impossible or must be done in terms of a privileged access to some transhistorical, God-like scheme.

A liberal society views freedom not as a transhistorical metaphysical value but as a condition under which such a piecemeal process of articulating, enacting, and justifying desirable practices and procedures takes place by relying on persuasion and not on force. Thus Rorty says that in an ideally liberal society the distinction between the reformer and the revolutionary is canceled out.[43] He quotes approvingly a passage from Dewey, who thought that philosophy can contribute to the emergence of such an ideal.

When it is acknowledged that under disguise of dealing with ultimate reality, philosophy has been occupied with the previous values embedded in social traditions, that it has sprung from a clash of social ends and from a conflict of inherited institutions with incompatible contemporary tendencies, it will be seen that the task of future philosophy is to clarify men's ideas as to the social and moral strifes of their own day.[44]

The Scope of Kant's Question

Kant's question "What can I know?"[45] was motivated by a quest for certainty. For historical reasons he sought answers that would deliver philosophy from the clutches of skepticism. Crediting Hume with having interrupted his dogmatic slumber, Kant embarked upon the task of rescuing philosophy from the skepticism into which it was plunged by that Scottish thinker when he followed out the logical consequences of Lockean empiricism and Cartesian rationalism. Kant wanted to show how we can have mathematical and scientific knowledge. He also wanted to preserve belief in freedom, immortality, and God from the skeptical consequences of theoretical reason. His quest for certainty led him to look for an indubitable foundation. He claimed to have found such a "datum" in the capacity of practical reason to set for itself universalizable goals, that is, goals of morality. He claimed that the immediate certainty of moral consciousness entitles us to postulate freedom, immortality, and God's existence.

The a priori structure of the mind guaranteed certain knowledge about nature, and the a priori character of the categorical imperative guaranteed moral knowledge. Although in Kant's philosophical system the thing-in-itself is not even a *candidate* for knowledge (it cannot be known but can only be thought), it is nevertheless accessible to us through moral experience. Its direct action is even extended in the direction of religion, entitling us to think of ourselves as inhabitants of the noumenal world as well. But it is to be noted that membership in that world is *practical,* not theoretically accessible, and as such it does not call for an epistemological analysis. The moral law does not give us any information, it only tells us what we ought *to do.*

19

By embracing a purely formal, transcendental test for moral action, Kant created notorious philosophical difficulties. To declare that epistemological certainty in the theoretical realm is incommensurable with practical certainty, or the moral demand, is to make empirical considerations irrelevant. Empirical knowledge has nothing to contribute to morality. What I know empirically has nothing to do with what I ought to do. Much of Kantian scholarship was spent on trying to make sense of this conundrum. Kant still insisted that particular moral maxims can be *derived* from the categorical imperative. He declared, for example, that the maxim of truth-telling is absolute. But this struck many critics as a dogmatic assertion, which makes it impossible to reconcile moral conflicts. Among the attempts to rescue Kant from his arbitrary absolutism was Marcus Singer's claim that Kant misunderstood his own theory and that in cases of conflict between two moral maxims—say, truth-telling and saving a life—one ought to apply the categorical imperative all over again.[46] This proposal, however, ultimately amounts to the admission that difficult cases require attention to all the relevant empirical details, and it is the nature of such details that will show *whether* the categorical imperative is applicable.[47] In other words, a good deal of concrete moral discernment is presupposed as preparation for the applicability of the formal test.

It is significant that in spite of separating human experience into two incommensurable realms—the theoretical and the practical—or in spite of regarding human beings as inhabitants of two worlds—the natural and the intelligible—Kant nevertheless tried to forge them into a unity. He did so by declaring the practical realm to be superior to the theoretical.[48] Since the moral, intelligible realm has the jurisdiction about what one ought to do and what one may hope, to the extent that human experience is unified the three Kantian questions can be seen as interrelated. For Kant, their interrelatedness stems from their being lodged in an essential human nature. That nature, however, can be fully revealed only after death.

Kant's postulate of the immortality of the soul was a way of providing an ultimate answer to the question of what or who we are. While embodied, we do not know how to answer that question with any degree of certainty, but after death we may discover our real nature. Acting as we ought, that is, living according to rationally derived moral laws, makes us *worthy* of happiness. The answer which

Kant gave to his third question was the result of his analysis of the nature of morality. Living according to rationally derived moral laws makes one worthy of happiness, but the deserved happiness, which Kant also calls "the systematic unity of ends," may escape a person in actual life. The reality of this unity is based, for Kant, on "the postulate of a supreme original good." "In a supreme good, thus conceived, self-subsistent reason, equipped with all the sufficiency of a supreme cause, establishes, maintains, and completes the universal order of things, according to the most perfect design—an order which in the world of sense is in large part concealed from us."[49]

Notice that the search for the foundations of knowledge leads Kant in the direction of his two other questions: "What ought I to do?" and "What may I hope?" To learn ultimate truth about themselves human beings need to act in certain ways and to entertain certain hopes. Kant's answer to the third question is based on a variant of a religious view that presupposes that there is such a thing as human nature, or essence, or ultimate destiny. In contrast to traditional religious views, he didn't claim to *know* anything about the concealed part of the perfect design which an immortal happy soul would encounter. Kant remained a skeptic about knowledge of any ultimate human destiny; beyond trying to live morally, one has no conception of the ultimate target of human hope.

The three Kantian questions are not, however, on a par; in his mind they appear hierarchically ordered. "What may I hope?" is ranked highest, since the answer to it will reveal a person's ultimate destiny, essential nature. "What ought I to do?" deals with the conditions of such a revelation, although the foundation of these conditions is a special "datum" which provides access to the moral law, the origins of which are shrouded in mystery. But this admission damages Kant's famous distinction between natural phenomena that *work* according to laws and human beings who *act* according to the conception of a law.[50] The knowledge of empirical facts as governed by natural laws is very different from the "knowledge" of the moral law, especially in the light of the admission that the source of that "knowledge" is noumenal, transcendentally mysterious. In resorting to this move, Kant merely exhibits his foundationalist ambitions, while nevertheless admitting that they cannot be philosophically articulated but must be sought in direct moral experience.

It is this kind of impasse that unites Cratylus, Parmenides, and Heidegger. Philosophy is either reduced to silence or to employing the pronoun "It" without a corresponding noun or to arguing for the conceptual equivalence of Being and Nothingness. Rorty recommends a way of dealing with this impasse. As Kant himself suspected, his three questions are interrelated, even though he chose to relate them, unsuccessfully, in terms of his foundationalist project. There are reasons to think that the idea of knowing makes better sense when it is seen under the umbrella of coping. Indeed, if we take a closer look at this rich pragmatic notion, we will discover that it inherently includes knowing, acting, and hoping; each aspect is integrally related to the remaining two.

Coping: Knowledge/Action/Hope

To discard the notion of knowledge as mirroring, or reaching down (or up) to some preexistent foundations, is to confirm Kant's suspicion that his three questions cannot be separated. Knowledge involves action, and action involves hope, and "coping" involves all three taken together. In a Heideggerian mood, one might speculate why "coping" normally takes the preposition "with." One is coping with a neighbor, or with a problem, or more globally, with experience or with the world. "Withness" suggests a fusion, a direct connection with the object of coping; it does not push us in the direction of postulating some independent reality to which coping, as a separable process, is somehow related. That is why it is perfectly natural to use the verb "to cope" without specifying an object. The philosophical advantage of this use is that it avoids the trap of such binary distinctions as appearance and reality, the knower and the known, subject and object, phenomena and noumena.

"Coping" acknowledges the "holistic" sense of our dealing (coping) with the world. The addition of "with the world" is unproblematic when "world" is used in a straightforward nonphilosophical sense, that is, prior to its being co-opted by the Kantian epistemology. (But even Kant, unlike Descartes, claimed that the self and the world arise *together*.) When we speak of the world in this unproblematic nonphilosophical way, the locution "coping with the world" easily accommodates all three dimensions treated separately in Kant's questions. Thus the world as the object of coping is something knowable, in which we act and entertain hopes. The target of coping is the world itself understood in this primitive, holistic sense.

By inviting us to look at knowledge through the metaphor of coping rather than copying, Rorty picks up the themes sounded ◊ by James, Dewey, and Wittgenstein, who viewed knowledge as *activity* rather than contemplation. This shift does not do away with the need to work with the "data" of experience—perception, observation, concepts, and theories. Nor does it deny the importance of establishing conclusions as "resting points" of what Kuhn has dubbed "normal science." But theories, for James, "become instruments, not answers to enigmas, in which we can rest. We don't lie back upon them, we move forward, and on occasion make nature over again by their aid."[51] The great use of laws of nature "is to summarize old facts and to lead to new ones. They are only a man-made language, a conceptual shorthand, as some one calls them, in which we write our reports of nature, and languages, as is well known, tolerate much choice of expression and many dialects."[52]

What Rorty's pragmatist predecessors emphasized was the *functional* role of funded knowledge—common sense and the results of scientific inquiries—in an ongoing process of successful adaptation to the contingencies and exigencies of experience. Like Wittgenstein, they saw the *forms* of such adaptations to be immersed in the stream of life.[53] Those forms have no independent ontological status apart from that immersion. They are being animated, kept alive and relevant, by the steady attention to how they function in the ongoing purposeful activity of human beings. Gilbert Ryle was pointing in a similar direction when he distinguished between knowing that and knowing how and emphasized the importance of "heedfulness" and improvisation in all thought.[54] When he suggested that what we call sensation should not be counted as a *mental* event,[55] he recognized, as did the pragmatists, that all *data* of experience, if they are to be a part of mental life, must be *taken up* in a process that is governed by criteria of success or failure and that aims at what James regarded as good in the way of belief, that is, true. Like Wittgenstein and like the pragmatists, Ryle recognized that normativeness is built into the very idea of knowledge.

If the pursuit of knowledge is animated by the concern for finding better, more adequate ways of coping with experience, then it is clear why Rorty joins Kuhn and Davidson in paying special attention to the role of "revolutionary science" and to changes of paradigms and metaphors. These constitute the cutting edge, the frontier area of thought and inquiry, the territory in which one is likely to encounter a scientific genius or a strong poet. But these "archetypal human beings"[56] differ from the rest of us only in degree, not in kind, inasmuch as every attempt at understanding and interpretation stretches any human mind in the direction of the still-unknown and problematic.

When we concentrate on the frontiers of present-day knowledge our thinking is bound to be "revolutionary," that is, not satisfied with the normal, criteria-governed body of beliefs. It will not be oriented toward closing off, firming up the beliefs already held. Consequently, the question "What can I know?," if it means "What can I reduce to firm, certain knowledge?," will not satisfy our intellectual needs. For it may direct us *away* from exploratory inquiries, not governed by a research program, not set to "nail things down."

Coping includes a strong interest in *advancing* knowledge, in helping it grow. To be sure, if we specify that subsumption under clear and distinct criteria is the only relevant test for knowability, then any and every aspect of experience can be *made* knowable— by laying down such criteria. In such situations we can be said to know, that is, to have succeeded in providing a set of criteria in terms of which some segment of phenomena can be understood. We are entitled to claim knowledge when we become familiar enough with the phenomena in question and have no cause to suspect the presence of anomalous cases. Here we are in the territory of "normal science" or conventional morality, allowing us to make reliable knowledge claims.

Undoubtedly, the more we learn about a phenomenon, the more criteria can be established for dealing with it intelligently. And this is what we do in common sense and in science when we resort to descriptions of familiar natural facts by citing laws of nature or to justifications of actions by adducing generally accepted moral rules. But these "normal" or "familiar" areas of discourse still leave much room for the exercise of intelligence that does not terminate in knowledge as above specified but instead calls for breaking new ground in our efforts to cope with the unfamiliar, with phenomena unexplained by accepted theories. The task we are facing calls for forging new tools, which *may* possibly become useful in producing future knowledge but on the other hand may not. There are situations where we feel the need to introduce new vocabularies and to invent new paradigms for which as yet there is no room in received theories, beliefs, and criteria. Furthermore, and more importantly, if the new metaphors take hold, the epistemological status of these theories and beliefs is likely to change as well, enabling us to view experience and nature in new, unforeseen ways.

Thus even in the empirical realm Kant's question "What can I know?" needs to be amplified by such questions as the following: "How can things be redescribed so as to put us in touch with aspects we are overlooking?" or "Which features in the familiar descriptions call for the enlistment of playful imagination and of novel linguistic experimentation?" To stop short of such amplifications is to limit oneself to already familiar explanations and theories, to "tried and true" paths, thus diminishing the likelihood that fresh perceptions and perspectives will emerge. We need to amplify the question by shifting from metaphors of finding to metaphors of making.

If the desire for success in coping enlists creative, innovative efforts on the part of human beings, it is not surprising that Rorty sees change in self-image as directly connected with the purposes of inquiry. Curiosity about the way the world works merges with the desire to explore the limits of what one can be, since one's being is coextensive with what one believes and desires. In that sense the human self is never completed as long as it keeps gaining in experience and understanding—which usually covers no less than a lifetime. But even a lifetime is not enough if one hopes that the process will continue in the careers of subsequent generations. It is this connection of knowledge with human growth that provides a justification for resorting to the label "humanistic pragmatism" to characterize the point of view that Rorty shares with his philosophical predecessors.

The notion of coping is likely to enlarge the scope of exploratory activity and spread it more widely among all kinds of intellectuals, that is, people whom Rorty defines as those who worry about their final vocabularies.[57] If there is no common grid from which one must start, one can concentrate on the particular position, viewpoint, orientation, and field of expertise one happens to be in. Thus, the reactive and edifying work, sending the conversation off in new directions, is distributed democratically among all persons who have the need and the determination to cope with their worries. This is the way in which philosophy becomes democratized.

Experience is an unending series of attempts at self-creation, both on personal and social levels. Our beliefs and our theories are the forms of our being. Their change and growth make up the history of the human career in its civilized stage. A break with the Platonic bias amounts to a kind of liberation, eloquently defended by John Dewey in some of his occasional lyrical flights.

> 'Reason' as a noun signifies the happy cooperation of a multitude of dispositions, such as sympathy, curiosity, exploration, experimentation, frankness, pursuit—to follow things through—circumspection, to look about at the context, etc., etc. . . . Reason, the rational attitude is the resulting disposition, not ready-made antecedent which can be invoked at will and set into movement. The man who would intelligently cultivate intelligence will widen, not narrow, his life of strong impulses while aiming at their happy coincidence in operation.[58]

It is this broadly humanistic consequence of pragmatism that Rorty finds congenial and with which he would like to join forces.[59]

What Ought I to Do?

The Task of Self-Creation

If there is no Essential Human Nature, each person faces the task of self-creation. The quest for determining what one can be and do is affected by the fact that Nature or Reality has no essence either and that our understanding of it keeps changing as we continue to devise new vocabularies and new theories. Fresh discoveries of what the world contains among its actualities and possibilities modify the appraisal of our powers and limitations; a change in knowledge may bring about a change in self-knowledge, and hence in motivation.

The notion of coping has something in common with what Heidegger called care, *Sorge*. One need not accept his metaphysical views in order to appreciate his phenomenological commentary on human existence. *Sorge* captures the basic mood (*Stimmung*, attunement) of being concerned, interested, involved, engaged—a condition to which American pragmatists also called attention. Heidegger contrasted this state of being with "inauthentic" ways of being, such as anonymity (*das Man*), idle talk (*Gerede*), and promiscuous curiosity (*Neugier*)—three typical forms of unfocusedness and distraction, characterizing much of average everyday existence. The Heideggerian distinction between different ways in which one may experience life—the distracted and diffused versus the concentrated and focused—was anticipated by Nietzsche in his omnibus phrase "God is dead." He used that phrase as a shorthand for the phenomenon of ennui, boredom which sets in when cultural values—ideas and ideals—get used up, transformed into dead metaphors, into all-too-familiar clichés. Nietzsche deplored such nihilistic tendencies and proclaimed his doctrine of the Overman and self-overcoming to spur the lagging human spirit on to new exertions, to novel creative endeavors.

If there is no Secret or Truth about nature or human nature, then the aim of self-creation is the task of devising particular ways of being "good at being human."[1] The contingent facts of the particular person's history form the setting for this task. Rorty credits Freud with having given due weight to contingent factors in the task of self-creation. According to Rorty, "Freud himself eschewed the very idea of a paradigm human being. He did not see humanity as a natural kind with an intrinsic nature, an intrinsic set of powers to be developed or left undeveloped."[2] Freud "leaves us with a self which is a tissue of contingencies, rather than an at least potentially well-ordered system of faculties."[3]

There is some plausibility in saying that what is aimed at in self-creation is akin to the work of art. What we become is the result of crafting a response to our idiosyncratic contingencies and possibilities. The materials of our experience are shaped into particular forms by our choices, some of which in time crystallize into character traits. Our psyches react to the actions and personalities of others—parents, siblings, teachers, and actual and imaginary heroes, villains, and models. Many significant events in our lives flow from our reactions to accidental encounters with other people and to unpredictable situations. We define ourselves in the process of meeting or failing to meet challenges put in our path by human and nonhuman circumstances. Thus, the resulting personality is something made, a work of art.

Rorty finds this assimilation attractive and, siding with Nietzsche, Freud, Harold Bloom, and Alexander Nehamas, is inclined to see the self as an "aesthetic consciousness," in addition to being a product of time, chance, and historical/political circumstances.[4] But perhaps a more modest, more realistic account is preferable. "Art," after all, is an honorific term. Not everything that is made deserves to be called "artistic" or "aesthetic." Perhaps the analogy can rightly apply to some exceptional human beings, but not to the common

28

run of us. If all of us are poets in self-creation, only some are strong poets, in Harold Bloom's sense.

Still, the assimilation of human personality to something made or created rather than found or discovered is on the right track and only needs a more modest description. In looking for such a description, we may make use of two helpful words, one French, one German. By *bricolage* the French mean something that is put together with a degree of ingenuity and success out of a medley of materials that does not lend itself to neat, elegant organization or packaging. Up to a point it is hodgepodge, contrived, improvised. The German verb *basteln* similarly connotes the process of putting things together out of ordinary, easily available materials, not covered by technological know-how. Yet what emerges in this process, which in English could be called "tinkering," is something that has a definite, particular character and can be valued for its own sake, without aspiring to the status of a work of art. Perhaps we can view a human self as such a *bricolage, etwas Gebasteltes,* arrived at by the modest means and talents at our disposal. This view may be more realistic precisely because the materials out of which we fashion our selves or souls are so heterogeneous, unpredictable, and often surprisingly, even implausibly, governed by the nonlaws of contingency.

When we refrain from characterizing our actions in terms of familiar Greek or Christian virtues and vices and instead scrutinize these actions in the Freudian vocabulary of "infantile," "sadistic," "obsessional," or "paranoid," we can become aware of aspects of behavior that the familiar terms either hide, obscure, or distort. With these additional descriptive/evaluative terms at our disposal, we are able to produce different, perhaps more accurate and more helpful accounts of ourselves. These accounts seem "more finely textured, far more custom tailored to our individual case, than the moral vocabulary which the philosophical tradition offered us."[5] The new vocabulary helps us to see more clearly that, since our pasts are particular and idiosyncratic, so are our attempts at self-creation.

Although not necessarily gifted poets in self-creation, all human beings resort to new metaphors to the extent that they generate some original, brand-new fantasies, some uniquely personal ways of viewing and reacting to the contingencies of experience. Every life is "an attempt to clothe itself in its own metaphors."[6] Rorty's view of human selfhood is not elitist; it includes everyone. He tells us that what poets do with their words, others can do with their lives, "with their spouses and children, their fellow workers, the tools of their trade, the cash accounts of their businesses, the possessions they accumulate in their home, the music they listen to, the sports they play or watch, or the trees they pass on their way to work." Human beings acquire a sense of self-identity from such multiple arrays of responses and activities, and Rorty credits Freud with having shown how that sense is "dramatized and crystallized."[7] Rorty also endorses William James's invitation to overcome the blindness that prevents us from seeing human lives as "private poems." Observing back-woods farmers clearing land for cultivation, James wrote as follows:

> I had been losing the whole inward significance of the situa-tion. Because to me the clearings spoke of naught but denuda-tion, I thought that to those whose sturdy arms and obedient axes had made them they could tell no other story. But when they looked on the hideous stumps, what they thought of was personal victory. . . . In short, the clearing which to me was a mere ugly picture on the retina, was to them a symbol redolent with moral memories and sang a very paean of duty, struggle and success.
>
> I had been as blind to the peculiar ideality of their conditions as they certainly would also have been to the ideal-ity of mine, had they had a peep at my strange indoor academic ways of life at Cambridge.[8]

Whether in Cambridge or in a virgin forest, the challenge of living, of noticing things that might have a bearing on what is worth doing, is no less difficult or less demanding. In responding to posi-tive or negative factors affecting our lives, we must draw upon all the energies available to us—physical, psychological, emotional, and in-tellectual. As Freud insisted, some of these energies may be uncon-scious, which prompted Rorty to remark that if we put a conformist on a couch, "we will find that he is only dull on the surface."[9]

Existentialists of various stripes have popularized the slogan that human existence puts itself in question. When looked at more closely, this dictum appears to be a modern version of Socrates' fa-mous saying: "The unexamined life is not worth living." Both statements reflect the acknowledgment of the contingency of life. For a being that lacks a definite, predetermined function, every item entering consciousness—from the outside or the inside—comes with a question mark: What about it? Should I ignore it? Should I do something about it? How shall I respond to it? Consciousness asks such questions because it does not know ahead of time what to make of life's contingencies; it cannot look up a blueprint prescribing how to behave in a given situation. There is no "it" putting itself in question because what that "it" becomes depends on the kind of answers the consciousness will come up with. This is what self-creation amounts to.

Dangers of Self-Creation

The word "creation" has a positive ring. When speaking of self-creation we tend to think of it as aiming at something good, something that has worth. But there is no guarantee that self-creation will move in that direction, that the "good" side of human nature will prevail in the end, the way John Stuart Mill expected the truth to prevail in its contest against all those who would keep it down.[10] Very different alternatives may also appear attractive to some human beings. In a startling analysis of Orwell's *1984*,[11] Rorty throws intriguing light on O'Brien's motivation, which had appeared puzzling and unconvincing to many astute readers and interpreters of that utopian novel. In the character of O'Brien we have a vivid and scary picture of a person whose self-creation results in a being who enjoys inflicting exquisite pain. O'Brien delights in his ability to destroy the mind of a person by destroying the capacity to form a coherent self. When he makes Winston believe that $2 + 2 = 5$, his objective is to break Winston's mind to pieces. "Getting somebody to deny a belief for no reason is a first step toward making her incapable of having a self, because she becomes incapable of weaving a coherent web of belief and desire."[12]

When O'Brien forces Winston to say, "Do it to Julia!," that is, to agree that rats should eat her face, he makes it morally impossible for Winston in the future to justify himself to himself. After uttering these words he can never reconstitute himself. And it is this self-knowledge on Winston's part that constitutes his torture, the torture which O'Brien enjoys to cause and to witness. O'Brien uses his power for the sake of witnessing such torture, not for the sake of building an egalitarian society. Thus, it is not O'Brien's philosophy, his political theory that explains his action, but rather the contingent fact that he happens to desire torture for its own sake.

The possibility that such human beings can emerge, with such motivation, is also among our contingencies, concludes Rorty. Nothing among the facts of human nature as we know it precludes this possibility. It may happen that people with O'Brien's motivation will find themselves in a position of power, enabling them to act out this kind of motivation, their boots grinding into human faces forever. A torturer can also be an intellectual at the same time. In fact, understanding, the ability to reason, to seek support and confirmation in the judgment of others, may be a necessary condition for this kind of torturer to derive enjoyment from what he is doing. He may at least appear to act like an intellectual, like a person who supposedly confirms his victim's rationality, precisely in order to destroy the victim's mind when an opportunity arises.

Rorty suggests that wielders of totalitarian power may include O'Brien-like characters, who merely, perhaps self-deceivingly, pretend to serve their political cause but in fact have become thugs and criminals. He wants to warn us about such a possibility, without entertaining any philosophical theory about human nature or human history. Who is to claim confidently that we need not be concerned about guarding against such contingencies? Rorty takes Orwell's *1984* to be a warning that such scary, frightening developments *are* within the realm of possibilities. Throughout its history, humanity has manifested countless instances of cruelty to its own kind—massacres, bloodshed, enslavement. It is gratuitous to dismiss or explain away such instances as aberrations or lapses caused by ignorance or temporary insanity. Deliberate slaughter of women and children, wholesale destruction of human lives, may have as a part of their context certain long-standing animosities and tribalistic hatreds, but a repeated willingness to participate in such crimes on the part of otherwise civilized human beings is not comforting. The state of mind attributed by Solzhenitsyn to his imaginary Stalin in *The First Circle* is not implausible.

Among the possible options for future humanity is that those who would gain power *might* want to use it the way O'Brien did. Rorty takes seriously Orwell's warning that the emergence of O'Brien types who would embrace the slogan that the purpose of torture is torture is not ruled out by anything in the nature of things. If one could be sure that those who succeed in capturing power over others would ultimately use it to create a decent society, then one would at least have an excuse to tolerate a temporary surrender of power to totalitarians. If the disagreement is only about the means and not the ends, the situation would not be hopeless. But nothing guarantees that those who gain power would not choose O'Brien's path.

The danger to which Orwell points in the character of O'Brien is not made impossible or unlikely by anything we know about human nature, and Rorty thinks that Orwell's importance in part rests on his warning us of this possibility. The destruction of Winston's mind by O'Brien is so horrible because it shatters our optimistic confidence that the human race cannot ultimately succumb to radical evil. But O'Brien is radically evil because after his "treatment" Winston could no longer accept himself; he is destroyed as a person. As Rorty suggests, if he were made to believe temporarily that $2 + 2 = 5$, when the cause of that belief were to be removed, he could say to himself: "I believed then that $2 + 2 = 5$." This item of self-knowledge would not be enough to preclude the possibility of recovery, especially if he were to come to understand that his rational capacity had been temporarily suppressed or turned off. This is what he would *have* to say to himself in order to go on trusting that he is once again in control of his beliefs. He would reject the belief that $2 + 2 = 5$ because this belief does not fit with the rest of his beliefs, in this case the beliefs about arithmetic as a coherent set of propositions. People believe in their own rationality based on the confidence that they have command of some set of logically connected propositions, that they can find their way among propositions that are presented for inspection, calling for assent or rejection.

The proposition that was meant to destroy Winston's mind concerned not only a set of beliefs which in part demonstrated his rational competence but also reached down into the set of beliefs that were *morally* relevant. Because Winston could no longer reconstruct himself morally after realizing that he actually said, "Do it to Julia!," that bit of self-knowledge destroyed him as a person in his own eyes. Winston could no longer accept himself; his self-respect was obliterated and he did not trust his own judgment any more. He was conscious of having done something so abhorrent that his self appeared to him irrevocably shattered into fragments that could not be put together to form a defensible whole. His own mind did not make sense to him any more.

Winston's case alerts us to the fact that the process of self-creation cannot be devoid of a concern for the well-being of others. Winston's mind was destroyed because he could not countenance himself as behaving the way he did toward Julia, the mitigating circumstances notwithstanding. In the light of this fact, the question "What ought I to do?" can hardly avoid the territory of morality.

The Role of Morality

Considerations we call "moral" appear as soon as the process of self-creation runs up against the question: Do my actions help define me alone, or do they help define humanity? Morality comes into being when one opts for the second alternative. To choose morally is to regard our individual choices as choices on behalf of others. From time immemorial moralists and founders of religions have repeatedly made this point, illustrating it by countless stories and parables. Among more recent versions of this claim are those proposed by Kant, Dostoyevsky, and Sartre. Kant's and Dostoyevsky's versions take the form of a moral or a religious exhortation: See to it that your choice be *good* for others! In the case of Sartre it is something less than that—a reminder, perhaps, that the free choice we make may trigger similar free choices by others. What is common to all such warnings is, however, that they acknowledge the distinction between the personal and the communal. What one chooses for oneself may not necessarily be good for others.

This distinction, however, works both ways. What one chooses for oneself need not be necessarily *bad* for others. When this is the case, that is, when nothing detrimental to others occurs as a result of an action, that action may be worth doing. A choice may look attractive to an individual without its being evident just how that choice may contribute to other people's quest for self-definition and self-fulfillment. Something may be good for an individual without necessarily being good *or* bad for others. In other words, a choice can be prudent, that is, contribute to the enhancement of the chooser's self-image, without raising the question of morality at all, when by morality is meant the taking into account the well-being of others. Of course, if the choice in question entails *harm* to others, moral considerations become relevant and it is no longer the question of prudence alone. But when this qualification is not in order, prudential considerations of the agent provide sufficient justification for action.

The prudence/morality distinction is useful when it is intended to call attention to the difference between being concerned and not being concerned about the needs or interests of others. But that distinction is not equivalent to the distinction between a private ethic of self-creation and a public ethic of mutual accommodation, which, according to Rorty, Freud wanted to draw.[13] Furthermore, it should be noted that moral deliberation is not always difficult and prudential calculation easy. The question "What ought I to do?" can be just as weighty and important when it is addressed to the uncertainty about the kind of person one is becoming as when it is centered on how others may be affected by the contemplated action. Indeed, one might argue that the concern about self-creation is more fundamental because it helps define, among other things, what the eventual relationship to others *is to be*. To deny the distinction between prudence and morality is to be motivated by the acknowledgment that the question "What ought I to do?" may sometimes have urgency and importance even though no moral claims are relevant at that time.

This sense of importance and urgency could not surface in the consciousness of the deliberating person unless there was an antecedent concern about the kind of person that is being created by the envisaged act. And if so, there is room for the verb "ought" even though it is not, or not yet, equated with the *moral* "ought." Thus, when a person decides "I ought to do *X*," he or she may be announcing a verdict which the project of self-creation yields in this particular context. Both the moral and the more general use of "ought" are used normatively, and in either case may function as a performative "Let me do *X*." That performative may appear unconditional. According to Rorty, Freud has shown that any seemingly random constellation of things "can set up an unconditional commandment to whose service a life may be devoted—a commandment no less unconditional because it may be intelligible to, at most, only one person."[14]

It is important to blur the distinction between prudence and morality because in this way the question "What ought I to do?" receives a more generous scope. It *can* be meaningfully asked in situations in which explicitly moral questions do not arise, and it allows of answers that take into account the idiosyncratic position of the person asking it. Its background may be the entire spectrum of resources available to a person engaged in self-formation, which may include talents and capacities that do not yet know their limits nor their precise application. In other words, it gives full sway to the powers of creativity and invention that need to be employed in order to reach toward human possibilities still unexplored. This kind of orientation is handicapped by the assumption that there already exists an essential human nature which limits individual aspiration.

Freedom and Tolerance

Under what circumstances can one expect the process of self-making, of giving a shape to who one is, to proceed in an optimal fashion? If there is anything that deserves respect, it is the human struggle to give meaning to its own existence. The task of self-creation must be seen as something *important,* different from all other known events and processes going on around us. One manifestation of respecting it is the willingness to let it proceed unimpeded, not to put in its path obstacles that would interfere with the attempts of human selves to make something worthy of themselves. This is where the question "What ought I to do?" moves into the social and political dimension.

Freedom, says Rorty, is "the recognition of contingency."[15] Its special role in the task of self-creation can be made clear when the point is put negatively. Energies at our disposal are diminished and depleted when in addition to the formidable task of sorting out and responding to life's contingencies we must also pit ourselves against constraints put on us by oppressive and intolerant social and political conditions. The work of developing into self-responsible and self-reliant persons is impeded when it is forced into rigid grooves and patterns or when it is hampered and paralyzed by pressures of social intolerance. The harm done occurs at the deep level of personal, idiosyncratic desires that are ignored, bypassed, or disconcerted by being immediately deflected from their initial course and channeled in the direction imposed by forces external to these desires.

Conditions of unfreedom and intolerance are of course to be distinguished from conditions conducive to making ourselves into beings we can respect. Self-respect-enhancing factors include moral guidance and discipline, which, especially in the early stages of personality formation, make the difficult work of autonomous self-creation easier. They make it easier because along with other virtues, such as the strength of character to deal with adverse circumstances, they also promote respect for freedom and tolerance as values *that make room* for self-creation. They provide conditions under which people can develop into confident and competent individuals, some of whom may indeed become works of art, worthy of admiration and emulation.

In Rorty's view, the Humean account of the human self as a centerless network or concatenation of beliefs and desires is perfectly satisfactory. It allows us to avoid the traditional tendencies to ascribe to human beings some deeply metaphysical powers, which in turn are seen in relation to other transcendentally interpreted realities, as is the case in Plato's account of the soul and in Kant's story about the higher noumenal self. Although the Humean view may look suspiciously reductionist or atomistic, Rorty's view of it does not encourage this conclusion. His main concern is to lead us away from the notion that what characterizes human beings is the possession of some central faculty called "reason" that presides over the task of character formation, of sorting out beliefs, directing desires, and determining choices. This picture is closely connected with the notion of Essential Human Nature, serving as a tribunal in which our beliefs and desires are judged and validated. While questioning this picture, Rorty does not think that its rejection entails the denial that among our desires there is one that consists in wanting "to make something worthwhile of ourselves, to create present selves whom we can respect."[16]

The desire to make sense of one's experience, to bring into it a degree of coherence, unity, and character, is not a function of some preexistent universal structure within, but it does not acquiesce in allowing contingencies to roam free, uninspected and untouched by one's psyche. If this were the real state of affairs, contingency would amount to a kind of uncontrollable indeterminacy, out of which no poetry or intelligibility could possibly emerge. If we were to ascribe such an internal "freedom" to ourselves, we could not make sense of what is happening to us or what we are doing.

Contingent relations, impinging on one's psyche from within or from without, are candidates for inclusion in one's self-image as at least a web, not an inchoate concatenation of unregistered and undigested happenings, without any significant relation to a person's beliefs and desires. To act out our idiosyncratic fantasies and metaphors, to exploit them for symbolic purposes, we need to respond to them, consciously or unconsciously, and to inspect editorially their admittedly contingent entry into our lives for possible clues as to what we are or would like to be as persons.[17]

We have the capacity to look at ourselves as something at least potentially worthwhile, something we can respect. That capacity is not just a theoretical desideratum but is also a practical prescription that exists alongside our awareness that we are at the mercy of contingencies invading our lives. As independent nonhuman events, contingent occurrences cannot be appropriated and transformed. But our *awareness* of them, generating metaphors and poetry, can amount to a sort of power over the world. So while we cannot affect the occurrence of contingencies, we can hope to face them, at least up to a point, on our terms. Coming to terms with contingencies is taking them up into the purview of one's beliefs, desires, hopes, and expectations, thus putting them into relation with something which in time becomes a person's more or less stable character which tries to deal with contingencies in terms of its own self-image.

Rorty recognizes that since attempts at self-creation are likely to be diverse and not always mutually reconcilable, they are therefore not always relevant to public and political matters. The quest for private bliss or perfection, which includes religious beliefs and philosophical theories about ultimate reality or the human self, is something that should be separated from the quest of establishing a just society. It so happens that democratic revolutions in the West have produced versions of liberal democracy in which institutional and procedural defense of freedom and tolerance have allowed the individual quest for perfection to flourish to a great extent. The emergence of such political systems is, however, not guaranteed by some ahistorical forces but is a particular achievement of particular societies developing under contingent historical conditions.

The private spiritual liberation, which Emerson thought to be characteristically American, occurred as a result of what Rorty calls disenchantment or de-divinization of nature and human nature. He uses these terms to describe the gradual weaning away from conceptions which represented reality in theological or metaphysical terms articulated in religious doctrines and philosophical schools, including such a progressive movement as the Enlightenment. Rorty credits Jefferson with having helped "make respectable the idea that politics can be separated from matters of ultimate importance," and having succeeded in convincing the other Founding Fathers that it is best "to privatize religion, to view it as irrelevant to social order but relevant to, and possibly essential for, individual perfection." [18]

Unlike Michael Sandel, Rorty thinks that the notion of a contingent, "radically situated subject" is sufficient for the justification of liberal democracy. In his opinion, it is better not to talk about the self as something that *has* beliefs and desires. If we start with the notion of a substantive self, we then endow it with the capacity to choose ends. This is what Sandel does when he says that "this capacity is located in a self which must be prior to the end it chooses." [19] Indeed, the very idea of *justifying* liberal democracy by reference to some metaphysical self is of dubious use to upholders of democratic institutions precisely because it shifts attention from the pragmatic function of these institutions to metaphysical arguments which, not appearing convincing to every supporter of democratic procedures, may nevertheless undermine the commitment to these procedures. Such metaphysical arguments should be relegated to contexts in which philosophically inclined persons seek personal perfection through such reflection.

It is historically true that the democratic state was helped into existence by such arguments as that on behalf of universal human rights, but Rorty does not think that a democratic society is contingent upon acceptance of such "absolutist" claims addressed to humanity at large. Commitment to liberal democracy is "something relatively local and ethnocentric—the tradition of a particular community, the consensus of a particular culture,"[20] which happens to have established institutions promoting freedom and tolerance. The existence of such institutions does not show that "community is constitutive of the self," a position taken by "communitarian" theorists, such as Robert Bellah, Alasdair MacIntyre, Charles Taylor, and Michael Sandel. Rorty doubts that liberal democracy needs any such philosophical justification or "anthropology" but grants that the language of rights and common purposes can help articulate democratic ideals and comports well with them.[21] Those who embrace such ideals have come to regard justice as the first virtue of a political state, while being "as indifferent to philosophical disagreement about the nature of the self as Jefferson was to theological differences about the nature of God."[22]

Rorty does not regard his view about the contingency of democratic states as idiosyncratic. He sees it supported by the writings of John Rawls, who also, according to Rorty, "wants views about man's nature and purpose to be detached from politics."[23] Ultimate beliefs, held on religious and philosophical grounds, should not be subject to legal coercion, and discussions of social policy should be disengaged from such beliefs. This will not prevent a democratic state from using force against individuals who threaten its institutions by appeal to such philosophically or religiously grounded conscience. Commitment to democratic institutions may be serious even if democracy is not rooted in human nature. To support this conclusion Rorty cites Joseph Schumpeter: "To realize the relative validity of one's convictions and yet stand for them unflinchingly is what distinguishes a civilized man from a barbarian."[24] Those who defend liberal democracy against its enemies do so not out of mere "preference" but because they are conscious of the losses entailed by surrendering control over their lives to people who do not take democratic institutions seriously. The worry about the consequences of such a surrender may set limits to tolerance, prompting the defenders of liberal democracy to take practical measures against those who would threaten its continuance and would therefore in that respect appear to be mad. "Accommodation and tolerance must stop short of a willingness to work within any vocabulary which one's interlocutor wants to use, to take seriously any topic which he puts forward for discussion."[25]

The Goals of Democracy

Faith in democracy is born out of repeated disillusionment with attempts to devise political systems that would provide a comprehensive blueprint of what ought to be done and by whom. As history has shown, such attempts to impose rigid control in all areas of human activity—economics, politics, science, religion, education, art—have brought much suffering to the human race, even though, as in the case of Plato's *Republic,* the intent was to appeal to the nobler impulses of humanity. Rorty joins those who encourage a disenchantment with or a de-divinization of such global projections of what is good for all human beings. Such projections are usually concomitants of a monistic, monolithic metaphysics, claiming to provide for everyone and for all situations definitive answers to the question "What ought I to do?"

Out of resistance to rigid political, social, and economic restrictions there emerge the key values of democracy: freedom and tolerance. According to Rorty, democracies have "helped to make the world's inhabitants more pragmatic, more tolerant, more liberal, more receptive to instrumental rationality."[26] Such a rationality, encouraging enterprising and innovative economies, has been effective in producing much material wealth, thus raising living standards for everyone, including the least advantaged. Democracies have increased literacy and stimulated the flowering of the arts. All along they have encouraged pluralistic cultures and peaceful coexistence of ethnic and religious traditions, thus serving as important vehicles of moral progress.

Freedom and tolerance, when embodied in institutions and general practice, provide private and public benefits. They put a premium on forbearance and noninterference with the self-images and legitimate pursuits of others. In the public realm they safeguard against harm by requiring compliance with democratically established laws. They encourage practices and activities based on respect for the freedom of conscience and the mutually recognized aspiration for well-being and peace of mind. Among the institutions fostering the attainment of such goals are education and free access to information.[27]

Democracy lives on voluntary experiments in cooperation. It thrives on the ethics of consultation, compromise, mutuality, and reciprocity. Reliance on such mechanisms of cooperation is learned in various contexts of participation and is not immediately appreciated by those who have become used to being handed down instructions of what they ought to do and why. When totalitarian regimes remain in power for a considerable time, they alter the expectations and motivations of their subjects. People accustomed to detailed instructions and guidance from politically controlled institutions find democratic experiments in cooperation unsettling and bewildering. Many emigrants from the Soviet Union have experienced this difficulty firsthand. They must give up the advantages of being guided and directed, which minimize the need for independent thinking, self-reliance in action, and adventure of ideas. In a free society, even if the rules and procedures are just and the opportunity to succeed equally available to everyone, success is not guaranteed.

There is also no guarantee that the participants in and the beneficiaries of a democratic political system will turn out to be admirable human beings. The capitalist system, although consonant with ideals of political freedom and economic free enterprise, is also open to distortions and abuses, leaving much room for injustice, corruption, selfish exploitation of power and wealth. According to Alasdair MacIntyre, the ethos of our culture is dominated by "the Rich Aesthete, the Manager, and the Therapist."

Not disagreeing with MacIntyre's observation that such character types can flourish in a democratic society, Rorty nevertheless suggests that we should see such phenomena against the background of positive gains.[28] Moreover, he takes a more charitable attitude toward the possibility of human failure. Commenting on a recent attempt to present humanity with a noble overarching vision, namely, that of Nietzsche's Overman, Rorty self-consciously takes on an approving stance toward the "last man," thought by Nietzsche to be the opposite of Overman, the "highest" human type. This stance may suggest that democratic societies have no higher aim than what he (Nietzsche) called the "last man"—the people who have "their little pleasures for the day and their little pleasures for the night."[29]

But the illocutionary force of this ironic twist of Nietzsche's doctrine is, I believe, to turn us away from high-handed pronouncements on what people ought or ought not to be doing with their lives. No one has enough wisdom to aim at the creation of a new brand of human beings, and therefore democratic societies should not aim "at anything less banal than evening out people's chances of getting a little pleasure out of their lives."[30] In virtue of evening out these chances, a free society will enable all its members to pursue their private visions of a good life. Not all such visions would produce good models to follow, but a democratic society would tolerate them in the spirit of Mill's *On Liberty*.

Whether democratic societies will prevail in the future is a contingent matter, and Rorty is not sanguine about their chances. But even if the future course of events should eliminate liberal democracies from the face of the earth, perhaps not all will be lost; "perhaps our descendants will remember that social institutions *can* be viewed as experiments in cooperation rather than attempts to embody a universal and ahistorical order." Rorty finds it hard to believe "that this memory would not be worth having."[31]

The Uses of the Past

The materials for self-creation, for adopting beliefs, commitments, purposes, and plans, come from one's social and political setting, from local culture. Personal identity is preceded by socialization, by the process of acquiring beliefs, values, and principles that describe the culture into which one is born. What that culture regards as moral, for example, gives expression to what it cares about and would like to see continued by the following generation. To the extent that a set of beliefs and commitments is taken seriously, it constitutes the culture's form of life, and as such is presented to the young as deserving respect and allegiance, imitation and emulation. As long as there is some vitality in the rules by which a group of people lives, they are candidates for being taken seriously, for constituting at least a partial personal identity on the part of the members of that group, especially the young generation.

Moral codes are crystallized forms of past creativity. They are passed on to the next generation as gifts of wisdom garnered by previous generations. They recommend the continuance of practices regarded as worthy and valuable, fair and decent. Nevertheless, a culture that has not become routinized and eviscerated is likely to acknowledge that its grasp of what is worth knowing and doing is not complete and must be open to unforeseen contingencies. So while it will try to teach and propagate factual beliefs and moral principles as they appear to provide guidance for already familiar contexts and situations, it will nevertheless acknowledge the possibility and the likelihood of circumstances under which the received wisdom will not be quite enough.

The relationship to the past will be perceived differently depending on one's attitude toward traditional rules. One may be *critical* of these rules because they do not cover successfully *all* of the contemporary circumstances. Or one may *honor* these rules as *partially* successful ways of handling problematic situations. And since it is often an open question as to how useful the old rules still can be, it will be premature and imprudent to dismiss them cavalierly as long as they can provide at least initial guidance. It is only fair to remember that the creators of old rules and values were projecting them in the hope that they would be more useful, more comprehensive, and more stable than they in fact turned out to be. It would be therefore both arrogant and ungrateful to turn one's back on, or to be dismissive of, what the tradition has to offer.

When Rorty recommends that systematic, criteriological discourse be supplemented by a reactive, edifying discourse, he does not suppose that funded knowledge and received wisdom are irrelevant to the quest for self-definition. As revolutionary science makes sense only against the background of normal science, and as the reach of new metaphors can take place only in the context of literal language, so attempts to decide what one ought to do must start with the awareness of the beliefs, ideals, and guidelines embedded in the tradition.[32]

Our relation to our tradition appears in a different light when we consider what attitudes we would like our descendants to take toward the values *we* hold. Commenting on Philip Larkin's poem, Rorty notes that many, if not most, poets regard their works as in some ways unfinished, that they haven't quite captured what they were trying to express; the possibility of completion depends on the kindness of strangers—future readers and poets. What goes for poets goes for anyone trying to arrive at some truth or to create something admirable; finality and completeness elude all mortal beings. So if there are some potential improvements in the projects that one leaves unfinished at the time of death, one hopes that they may be made by those who will come after us.

The hope that future strangers will be kind to us has a corollary. *We,* as strangers to those who lived before us, ought to be kind toward them. How? By being attentive to what they cherished and left unfinished—a vast territory indeed. That territory includes beliefs, values, and rules that we have inherited and that, in their general way, tell the story about aspirations and accomplishments in terms of which the human beings who preceded us tried to define themselves and to devise their forms of life. Approached in this spirit, traditions, institutions, moralities, and existing cultural artifacts will appear not as impersonal, abstract forms but as substantive human realities brought into existence by the creative energies of past generations.

The attitude appropriate to this kind of acknowledgment is described by the Polish poet Adam Asnyk in a stanza of his *Ode to Youth.* It captures the point I am trying to make and says something that everyone, not just young people, should take into account.

> But do not trample upon the altars of the past
> Even if you yourselves are to erect more magnificent ones,
> Because they are still aglow with holy fire
> And human love stands there guard
> And you owe them honor.

The attitude toward the past which Asnyk recommends is, however, not a reverence for something perfected, completed—an eternal verity. Rather, it is a declaration of solidarity, an acknowledgment of the continuity of our present efforts to form ourselves into beings we can respect with the efforts of our predecessors to accomplish the same objective. No civilization, no tradition, no system of ethics, no political structure, and no collection of works of art has captured all possibilities for good life and thus provided a uniform blueprint of what everyone ought to do. Therefore, no generation of human beings can dispense with the need to take into account the contextual contingencies, dangers, and opportunities that arise for them in their lifetime. While the proper and inescapable starting point for a process of self-definition is the set of current beliefs and values, the continuation of this process requires a critical and innovative stance toward these very beliefs and values at points where they might prove to be in need of modification, development, or radical revision.[33]

Writing as a Form of Coping

Among the creators of knowledge helping us cope are writers. The works they produce are divided into genres. There are advantages to dividing into disciplines the territory of what is worth knowing or commenting upon, but a dogged adherence to boundaries created by the classification into genres can result in distortions. Rorty has raised eyebrows among philosophers by suggesting that what they are doing is a form of literature, a kind of writing. This observation should not really be surprising in our time when interdisciplinary cooperation is gaining an ever wider acceptance, and when the boundaries between disciplines are increasingly blurred. The boundaries become less visible not because some disciplines are more effective in settling questions and therefore invite "poaching," but because concepts and approaches in one can be useful to another.[34]

If the object of investigation is not to discover a uniformly conceived correspondence to reality but instead represents various ways of coping with experience, then it is sensible to ask in just what ways this coping is successful. By suggesting that philosophical writing is a form of literature and by pointing to the philosophical effects of such "nonphilosophical" writers as Orwell, Rorty enables us to take a fresh look both at the motivation and the actual outcome of any given author's work. An interesting, and surprising, claim of his most recent writings is that while the motivation of a philosopher may be to describe reality, the actual accomplishment is the change in the way his readers perceive their subjectivity. Conversely, a piece of writing that is "merely" literary may in fact play a role in affecting social and political sensibilities, thus helping to bring about significant changes in social and political structures. Taking such actual effects into account, we may become more attentive to the idiosyncratic way in which a given piece of writing functions, without jumping to the conclusion that because it is within a certain genre, it *must* aim at or produce certain generally expected effects.

The division of writers into philosophical and nonphilosophical looks questionable to Rorty. When he suggests that Philosophy should give way to philosophy and when he recommends that all writing should be viewed as a seamless whole, he alerts us to the element of contingency that characterizes all human endeavor. A piece of writing can have motives and effects not predictable from the genre it follows. It all depends on what a given writer manages to convey as a result of being seized by a certain idea; even the writer may be mistaken in expecting only one kind of result when he or she is trying to work out a certain problem.

Thus, thinking of themselves as following out the implications of their tradition, thinkers may not realize that they are in fact undermining that very tradition, as Hume did in the case of empiricism. Or, believing that they are escaping their tradition, they may in fact be elaborating on it in some surprising ways. Kant, Peirce, Nietzsche, and Heidegger believed that they were putting an end to metaphysics, but in reality they were only producing alternative metaphysics. Even such a free spirit as Derrida, according to Rorty, still shows signs of lapsing into metaphysical ways.[35]

When it comes to estimating just what a given writer accomplishes, customary expectations may be misleading. We must pay attention to what actually transpires. Rorty claims, for instance, that the contribution of such writers as Nietzsche or Heidegger is not primarily to articulate a general conception of reality or to formulate a picture of the world as a whole—something we traditionally expect philosophers to do—but rather to give us useful material for our personal attempts at self-creation. What Nietzsche and Heideg-

47

ger are good at is forcing us to think in new ways about ourselves, but they are not good at all in telling convincing stories about ultimate reality. They did not draw proper conclusions from their own supposed demolition of metaphysics.

The talent for redescription is spread out across an entire spectrum of literary genres, and what is redescribed is not some preexistent reality but various ways of making sense of human experience in its multifaceted aspects. This is why Rorty recommends that we disregard the traditional division of writers into poets, philosophers, novelists, and scientists and instead pay attention to what they actually accomplish. The talent for redescription is distributed among such disparate writers as Pythagoras, Plato, Milton, Newton, Goethe, Kant, Kierkegaard, Baudelaire, Darwin, and Freud.

If we accept Rorty's recommendation that we should think of philosophy as just another form of literature, indeed that it is desirable to blur all genres of writing, we are likely to ask more precise and more helpful questions. We might ask, for instance, what the writer's actual objectives are, instead of presupposing that belonging to a genre answers this question automatically. Rorty concludes that Nietzsche and Heidegger, for example, aim not at beauty alone, that is, at a telling, revealing description of a temporal phenomenon, but also at sublimity, a successful expression of an eternal, unchangeable truth about temporal phenomena. But their search for sublimity seems so intense as to make them overlook or be indifferent to some important moral phenomena, for instance, human suffering. Like metaphysical theorists whom they criticize, such ironist theorists as Nietzsche or Heidegger still hope to come up with a final, universal truth about reality, without realizing that they merely provide a quasi-aesthetic satisfaction by providing new and startling descriptions, while losing track of the real effect their writings have on readers.

Rorty thinks that literary writers may be less prone to ignore human suffering because they are not preoccupied with the eternal but pay more attention to the temporal. For example, their writing may converge on the activities of a political liberal who regards cruelty as the worst moral vice.[36] Nabokov's concept of art includes curiosity as one of its components. According to Rorty, Nabokov's greatest works are accounts of artists who by concentrating on aesthetic bliss, and because of that concentration, are incurious about the suffering around them, including the suffering they themselves cause.[37]

The predicament of an honest writer, such as Nabokov, is the inability to accept aestheticism as sufficient justification for being an artist. There is no inevitable connection between artistic gifts and kindness. So artists cannot justify their lives by pointing exclusively to their artistic activity. But their *work* can also contribute to sensitivity to suffering by demonstrating the reverse, that is, how aesthetic creativity and artistic bliss can foster incuriosity about pain. In this way Nabokov's best novels sensitize the reader to pain without resorting to a theory. His contribution to political liberalism is in a sense greater than that of a theorist because the theorist does not work with tools that can make the suffering apparent. Only an artist can convert contingencies into moral insights, thus encouraging sensitivity to the objective of liberal politics.

What made Nabokov worry about his possible incuriosity about human suffering and doubt the moral value of his calling as an artist was a contingent fact about him and the time into which he was born. Aware of his father's direct involvement in attempts to diminish human pain, he created characters who, fascinated by the possibility of aesthetic bliss, bypass situations in which they could become aware of and possibly react to the fact of pain in others. And yet by depicting such characters Nabokov may have helped to sensitize his readers to such an awareness and reaction. In this way, Nabokov's special talents, possibly *because* of his personal moral doubts about himself, have made a contribution to the objectives of liberal democracy—to diminish pain.

Public Impact of Private Lives

An integral part of writing something down is that it can be communicated to others. A delightfully ironic demonstration of this fact is found in Dostoyevsky's Underground Man's "arguments" why he is putting on paper his paradoxical reflections about himself. He denies vehemently that he is trying to communicate anything to anyone or that he is trying to attract attention or that he is interested in having readers. He professes, implausibly enough, that his thoughts look better on paper, more dignified, more refined.[38] The Underground Man's ambivalence, feigned or real (Dostoyevsky's genius drops this puzzle nonchalantly into our laps), concerning his aims in writing may be emblematic of the difficulty of determining just how the boundary between the private and the public is established or maintained.

It is evident in what sense and for what reasons Rorty would like to keep the distinction sharp. His reasons, I believe, are moral. He wants to defend the right of individuals to be satisfied with being Nietzsche's "last men," with their "little pleasures for the day and little pleasures for the night," because he has respect for human beings' desire to choose their own mode of living. He wouldn't follow Nietzsche's way of whipping up people's ambitions to lift themselves by their own bootstraps to fulfill some, for them impossible, ideals. A part of this respect goes toward the recognition of human limitations and weaknesses, a humble and charitable attitude—toward others and toward oneself. In that sense, I believe, Rorty heeds some of the best impulses of our religious and humanistic traditions. There is a good deal of plain reverence for life, for letting things be. Santayana's similar sentiments come to mind here: "To love things spiritually, that is to say, intelligently and disinterestedly, means to love the love in them, to worship the good they pursue, and to see them prophetically in their possible beauty. To love things as they are would be a mockery of things: a true lover must love them as they would wish. For nothing is quite happy as it is, and the first act of true sympathy must be to move with the object of love toward its happiness."[39]

The limits of one's own powers are also ruefully recognized by another writer whose messages are "philosophical" even if communicated in a literary genre. What Conrad's Marlow admires in Kurtz is his ability to face his own death in a spectacular, "victorious" way. In contrast to Kurtz, Marlow describes his own weak, paltry way of facing the threat of death: "I have wrestled with death. It is the most unexciting contest you can imagine. It takes place in impalpable greyness, with nothing underfoot, with nothing around, without the great desire of victory, without the great fear of defeat, in a sickly atmosphere of tepid scepticism, without much belief in your own right, and still less in that of your adversary. If such is the ultimate wisdom, then life is a greater riddle than some of us think it to be."[40]

What a person ought to do, at a given moment, with his plans, or with his life, is first of all to be left up to that person. Such decisions are ineluctably private and, in a decent society, will remain so without hectoring or exhortation from the sidelines. There is a kind of "faith" in this injunction, a faith that could be called "humanistic" in the broadest sense of the word. That faith stems from the previously announced skepticism about the alleged preexistent essence of human nature. If there is no such essence, then one ought to let the energies of human life seek their own modes of fulfillment suitable to the self-conception of each individual.

This attitude also bears the implicit acknowledgment that we have no way of predicting the good that may emerge from the free contingencies of human experiments in living. The full significance of human exertions cannot always be evident even to the agents themselves. As Rorty suggests, Nabokov might not have been fully conscious of the political significance of his artistic motivation. Perhaps in his own way he was contributing to the causes that his father pursued by overtly political means. Likewise, Proust was, not necessarily consciously, settling scores with real people in his life, whom he "overcame" by redescribing them in his novels. And the magnitude of Orwell's contemplation of the possibilities of such an evil mind as O'Brien's alerted us to a scary interpretation of the urge to wield power over other human beings. Like Dostoyevsky, he saw human nature to be much broader than we thought, and he wished it were narrower. How to cope with Orwell's warning is a difficult question, but if the warning is not implausible, we are better off for having it presented to us in such an effective way in his novel.

Hegel's comment about grasping one's time in thought is not only normative, it is also inescapably descriptive. In Hegel's world view it had an implied reference to the Absolute Spirit hovering over world history. To resist that image is not to render the comment useless. Whether we like it or not, our times and our traditions claim and capture us, but in varying ways. The contingent facts of our birth, upbringing, education, and the events around us contribute to determining our grasp of what is happening and how it affects the fate of our community, nation, and region. What we make of our situation and our place in it is also a function of our abilities, propensities, and limitations, and to a not insignificant extent it depends on the choices we make in the process of defining ourselves and investing our energies. In all cases, we try to identify, or half-identify, the pinch of individual destiny, as William James has put it, or the blind impress of our behavings, as Philip Larkin has expressed it. Whether and to what extent these attempts or half-attempts satisfy us and lead to self-acceptance and peace of mind are hardly predictable and seldom controllable as we pursue our objectives and careers.

Yet, some of those careers, private as they essentially are, may nevertheless acquire a public relevance and, in rare cases, a larger significance. Which of them turn out to acquire this relationship is also to a large degree a matter of circumstances and blind chance, although special talent and proclivities in that direction are impossible to ignore and leave unrecognized. As Winston Churchill observed, history was going to be kind to him, because he intended to write it. Few of us can write even small chunks of it, but in limited and circumscribed ways all lives are somehow inscribed on public rolls even if these rolls are as large as those of voters or taxpayers. To be sure, the "public" significance of such participatory roles may not be high, but even the performance of such elementary public acts as voting and paying taxes gives the private person the status of a citizen. Participatory roles of a citizen in a democratic society are open-ended. A decision to run for a public office, for example, that of mayor or state representative, may launch a career that could affect thousands or even millions of lives.

Similarly, in the areas of intellectual endeavors, science, art, and other cultural affairs, most people populate the ranks of anonymous individuals, whose private metaphors never "catch on" and never enter the public domain. As participants in the adventures of science, for instance, we usually remain within its "normal" range, seldom privileged to participate even to a marginally competent degree in its "revolutionary" leaps. But occasionally an average freshman in a physics course may surprise himself and others by being later awarded a Nobel Prize: The stirrings of genius are usually recognized only in retrospect.

The interest in private talents *may* become a focus of public interest, and a society, if it is alert and wise, may make a claim on its creative individuals, especially when it deems their abilities useful for the solution of its important problems. Still, both the individual and society might ask whether the contribution sought could as well be made by others and, perhaps even more importantly, whether by demanding attention and commitment from *that* individual his or her other special abilities are being undermined or destroyed. It probably would have been a mistake for Nabokov to abandon his private literary career for the sake of pursuing causes to which his father devoted *his* life. Rorty's defense of the distinction between the private and the public appears to be motivated by his desire to allow people to choose their own life plans because no one should determine the destinies of others. This motivation is based on the hunch that the personal realm, in virtue of its originary, creative status, can and should absorb the attention and the energies of the individual, without its being automatically assumed that he or she has a moral obligation to make a contribution to whatever common ends are being pursued.

The values with which one starts, and what one does with them, cannot help but reflect one's social, cultural, and political setting. To what extent one's decisions and actions will have public impact is a contingent matter. Part of this contingency rests on the degree of solidarity with others that may emerge from the interaction between individuals and their communities. The extent and the weight of that solidarity are not only the result of deliberate design and planning; they are also an object of hope.

CHAPTER THREE

What May I Hope?

The Target of Hope

When Kant proceeded to answer the question "What may I hope?" it turned out that the target of his hope was something about which no *knowledge* could be had. Hope was to *take the place* of knowledge. Even the foundation of the answer to the question "What ought I to do?" lies outside the province of the question "What can I know?" Why morality interests us is a mystery; the categorical imperative is an a priori, something given prior to experience, a primary datum. In contrast, the pragmatic notion of coping *includes* the dimension of hope. According to Peirce (and other pragmatists as well), all meaning lies in the future.[1] To know the meaning of anything is to know what to do, what steps to take in order to find oneself in the presence of the intended object of thought. Peirce's famous one-page-long definition of lithium[2] illustrates his Pragmatic Maxim, according to which the perceptual and conceptual *consequences* of a term render its meaning. For William James, ideas are plans of action.

In general, the dimension of the future is included in any nonstatic theory of knowledge. To speak of verification, prediction, or control, even to raise skeptical doubts about the sun rising tomorrow, or to worry in general about the problem of induction, is to make the dimension of the future relevant, without necessarily suggesting that the explicit phenomena of hope can be encountered at the level of epistemology alone. As Wittgenstein pointed out, I do not hope that a yawning abyss will not open before my eyes every time I open the door of my house, nor am I seized by the emotion of eager anticipation when I say that I am expecting someone. But although it would be a mistake to look for typical phenomena of hope or expectation in such mundane goings-on when we are confident that we know what is the case, in the richer phenomena of coping, hope is a natural and normal ingredient.

Coping is not limited to the "matter of course" commerce with the world. As science needs to have "revolutionary" activity besides the "normal" one, so other dimensions of life call for something analogous. On the subjective, personal level it enters every case of an incomplete mastery of skill, technique, concept, or theory. We *hope* that we get things right, that we don't make mistakes, that we have not omitted some important steps, that we have grasped the point. On the objective, public level hope is present when we specify the conditions under which we expect our predictions to hold but hope that we have not overlooked some conditions that would wreak havoc with our predictions. Notoriously, this happens at the level of technology, but scientific laboratory experiments are also instances of technical or operational procedures. In the areas of law or social and governmental policy, the hope that, depending on one's motives and objectives, there are or aren't any loopholes in a statute or a regulation is a natural concomitant of one's expectations. Similarly, in the realms of morality or art it is difficult if not impossible not to bank on the trust, goodwill, cooperation, or collaboration of others.

When Rorty emphasizes the importance of the reactive, edifying, or hermeneutic side of intellectual life, he recognizes the dimension of hope as a prominent aspect of coping. In his view, hope is a vital ingredient of human life. He is critical of writers like Foucault who appear to leave no room for it in their analyses of our situation. He complains of Foucault's "inhumanism" and compares him unfavorably to Dewey, whose "vocabulary allows room for unjustifiable hope, and an ungroundable but vital sense of human solidarity."[3] He thinks that Dewey's "structures of culture," while acknowledging the need to include Foucault's "structures of power," also contain a provision that that structure is, at least up to a point, under human control. If we see social sciences as continuous with literature, we will have to grant that, like literature, they can contribute to "enlarging and deepening our sense of community."[4] There is an important difference between the use of social sciences as "instruments of domination" and of their use in what Dewey called "social engineering." The latter has room for hermeneutic and emancipatory actions and practices.

In contrast to both Hegel and Marx, Dewey "wants man and history to stand on their own feet, and man's history to be just that, neither Spirit's self-realization nor the fateful elephantine movements of Matter or of social classes."[5] Ideas are instruments of social change, and Rorty hopes that Dewey's piecemeal historicism will encourage social scientists to act in their explanations of cultures and texts "as interpreters for those with whom we are not sure how to talk." This is, he adds, "the same thing we hope for from our poets and dramatists and novelists."[6]

The Hope for Solidarity

If there were such things as an essential human nature and predetermined common destiny, and if humanity were to convince itself what they are, the result would be a uniform behavior governed by universal criteria. In the absence of such a common nature, human cooperation is always a matter of degree and the enlargement of it is only an object of hope. The kind of cooperation to be hoped and worked for Rorty characterizes as "unforced agreement." Among such unforced agreements are the practices of science and other activities in which the consensus on goals and procedures emerges from prolonged painstaking efforts to produce criteria governing a given practice. Those who participate in such activities do so because they subscribe to the values yielded by the consensus.

Since the theories and concepts explaining natural events and justifying human practices represent only some of the possible alternative options, namely, those that happen to have won out in the process of experimentation because they seemed optimal in answering to our needs and questions, Rorty recommends that we abandon the monopolistic notion of objectivity in favor of a more modest notion of solidarity. Although he does not explore in detail the neighboring conceptual territory of his semitechnical use of this word, it invites such an exploration. First of all, "solidarity," like "objectivity," has commendatory force. Since it connotes intersubjective agreement on some propositions, it could not be *contrasted* to objectivity, for in such an agreement some states of affairs are seen as holding for everyone. When a community comes to share a language, or when it follows a common practice, the very *existence* of such sharing or practice is a matter of objective fact. If the consequence of such a practice is successful coping, including prediction and control, the success of that coping is something objective, that is, can be repeatedly relied upon.

Rorty's notion of solidarity may be approximated when we combine Heidegger's two "existentials"—the characteristic modes of *Dasein: being-with* and *being-in.* Although solidarity primarily suggests "being-with," it also calls attention to "being-in," in the sense of coping successfully with some segment of the world, of moving effectively within it. Likewise, Wittgenstein's notion of the use of language as a technique, a practical mastery of some type of circumstances, may be suggested by Rorty's use of "solidarity." The notion of the form of life comes to mind here, especially when the stress falls not on "form" but on "life." Similarly, when Dewey's notion of "transaction" is purged of metaphysical connotations, it combines the subject-object relationship into a seamless whole, which seems to be present in "solidarity" as well.[7]

The rationale for preferring this term is that the unforced agreement is a function of consensual opting for a given vocabulary in describing a set of phenomena. In contrast to "objectivity," "solidarity" suggests flexibility and openness to change. As our vocabulary changes, so does our picture of the world. This flexibility (which Peirce connected with fallibilism) is likely to continue as long as the creative effort to improve our ways of coping continues. Unforced agreement is a state of affairs prevailing for a time when it is possible, as in "normal science," to invoke criteria which settle the question of what is the case, or what "the matter of fact" is. A claim is rational when it can be supported by such prevailing criteria. But, as Rorty points out, when the vocabulary of a field of inquiry is undergoing significant shifts, the rationality/irrationality distinction needs to be set aside, because such shifts cannot be evaluated in terms of criteria that were operative before the shifts occurred.[8]

The stepping-stones, the resting places of creative effort, are reached in the episodes of unforced agreement observed in any area of rational activity. The locus of unforced agreement is typically a local community or a tradition. But the locality need not necessarily or predominantly be physical, geographic. To be sure, the concreteness of interaction is more likely to be more evident in some geographical territory or when it is traceable historically, but the "locality" of the community may also be global, as is the case with science, world trade, and technological practices. Correspondingly, the identification of a person with a community reflects the particular character of that community and its specific scope. Although at a distance from one another, its members may think of themselves as "peers," adherents of a practice, participants in a tradition.

To emphasize the local aspect of a community or a tradition is also to remind oneself that it is not likely to be universally shared. The reasons for the limited scope of such a community are simply historical, not ontological. But it need not even occur to those who participate in such local forms of life and unforced agreements that there is anything relativistic about them. The question of universality or relativity does not even arise. The desire and hope for a wider acceptance of local forms of life may sometimes be present, and their merely "local" prevalence may be deemed regrettable. One may wish, for example, that the methods of science were more prevalent than in fact they are. With regard to other forms of life, however, one will not hesitate to admit the possibility and viability of alternative forms of life, even though for various reasons one may be unwilling to shed one's own.

All things considered, the bias toward one's own form of life is natural, which has something to do with the fact of our finitude. In the end, we must live our lives out of the resources available to us in our limited experience. This being the case, promiscuous switching from community to community, or an unrealistic stretching of our energies in too many directions, may signal either a lack of seriousness about any of one's chosen commitments or the presence of doubt about one's ability to devise an acceptable form of life. Normally, we do settle for some definite mode of conducting our life, and we acquire beliefs which make sense of it. When we do change our beliefs in a radical way, which may happen when we join another community, or choose an altogether different ambiance, the very conception of who we are and what makes sense changes as well. Such radical shifts are also shifts in solidarity. But it is natural to entertain the hope that one's chosen mode of life will prove sufficiently stable and solid, thus affording personal control and predictable satisfactions.

Solidarity and Change

Values by which people live are cultural artifacts and are generated by human groups in their particular historical setting. Solidarity *is* the experience of sharing a meaningful form of life. This form keeps changing as long as the culture is still vital, alert to new contingencies, which test the applicability and limits of criteria by which the fulfillments of that form are judged. Solidarity, however, is experienced not only when the criteria are being tested but also when they are unquestioningly enacted in the culture's normal practices—customs, celebrations, ceremonies, and rituals. Indeed, since the content of human cultures is rich, a product of centuries of previous creativity and invention, it is never the case that all of its treasures are mastered by any of its members. Because a culture's positive resources are in practice inexhaustible, those who live by them claim them as their own and cherish the opportunities to be fulfilled and renewed by them. An allegiance to a cultural group—an ethnic, national, religious, or professional identity—is usually suffused by the hope for its continuance. Subscribers to the values of a culture desire its perpetuation. This is true of allegiance to political traditions as well, and, according to Rorty, those who believe in it need not hope for more than its continuance.[9]

The vitality of cultural norms in part consists in their ability to provide *repeated* satisfactions. This expectation is not surprising because what to some has become a dead metaphor, to others is still communicating the freshness experienced by the metaphor's original creator. For this reason, education, as an introduction and initiation into a multidimensional culture, is usually regarded as an important activity for all members of the culture. Indeed, what we call "cultures" are particular networks of commonly followed rules and practices which are routinely accepted and habitually cherished by the members of the culture as *theirs*. The vitality of a culture in part depends on the degree to which the forms of life are experienced as meaningful and satisfying. Malaise occurs when a people—a culture, a civilization—no longer "identifies" with familiar, traditional values.

Because the relationship of a human group to its accumulated heritage is "vital," committed, supportive, and interested, and because that relationship is encapsulated in the language in which it is described, it would be somewhat misleading to compare language, as Rorty does,[10] to a coral reef in which the literal use of language (dead metaphors) is seen as the dead part of the reef, while new or metaphorical vocabulary is taken to represent the live, active part of the culture. The very idea of coping has built into it the possibility of making use of language and of other practices so as to further and to give adequate expression to people's changing interests and concerns. The intensity and the range of applications that a given form of life receives depend on what particular practitioners make of it under their individual conditions and circumstances. The "variations on the theme" that a given form of life may receive are as large as the number of individuals who are "governed" by that form. In this context, Wittgenstein's observation that we *let* ourselves be compelled by a form or rule is worth remembering.[11] The notion of use resists mechanization and is not reducible to automatic reactions.

Rorty is right in emphasizing the other component of the vitality of a culture, namely, the ability to create new metaphors, to depart from old meanings, to devise new vocabularies, and to forge fresh criteria. Human life feeds on this creative, "revolutionary," and edifying aspect of coping. Coping includes making originary moves—in language and behavior. However, the prominence of this aspect should not lead us to slight the processes of absorbing and appreciating practices and vocabularies already in place. Those who follow the inventions of poets, for instance, have to make an effort to approximate the experience the poet tried to capture in language. As Dewey observed, such an attempt requires attention and work. Although not original themselves, participants in innovations are enriched through the process of emulation. Emulation is not mindless imitation, for it involves an attempt to follow attentively a heretofore untrodden, unfamiliar path.

One might surmise that no culture has sufficiently and appreciatively absorbed all the treasures deposited in its history. Many a poet or a theorist has not become familiar enough; the *jouissance* of invention experienced by originators is not taken up by other potential experiencers of it. To that extent, it is *wasted.* One of the goals and hopes of a self-respecting society would be, therefore, to encourage acquaintance with originary metaphors and meanings that so far remain beyond the pale of many individuals. To foster such acquaintance is an acknowledged task of education, which in part contributes to the enrichment of students' lives by leading them in the direction of meanings that so far are unfamiliar to them.[12]

Metaphors get attention because they are *potentially* dead metaphors. But they become dead only after having had life. Their life is not limited to the moment of birth in the mind of their inventors, to the moment when they inexplicably appear, caused, say, by a cosmic ray. Before a metaphor dies it must attain some currency; it must cause *jouissance* in many experiencers, thus transforming to some extent their lives. Only when its flavor, its novelty, its freshness exhausts itself, does it get relegated to the familiar, commonsensical, ordinary. But the attention paid to it, and consequently its life, depends on the preparedness of the public to search for its possible meaning. Although not communicating any antecedent meaning, that is, not being proposed on the basis of criteria, it must at least be potentially meaningful, a *candidate* for meaning. To die, a metaphor must be capable of dying, hence first of all of *having* life.

The hope that individuals will participate in and benefit from the creation of metaphors is not likely to be fulfilled in a society dominated by a mass ethos. Mass ethos is bent on reaching as many people as possible in the shortest possible time. Where such an ethos prevails, the absorption of a new practice, fashion, or idea is not oriented toward the particular qualitative phenomenon of newness but rather toward the fact of its being eagerly absorbed by others. The focus of interest is not the objective novelty as such; one does not pay attention to its intrinsic character but merely to the fact that it is being shared with others. This may be a reason why those caught up in such a mass mentality easily fall into ennui, boredom.

By not paying attention to the *target* of new creative efforts (as distinguished from following fashion, the "taste" of the crowd), a person is not likely to benefit from original insights and inventions. Not in possession of informed judgments about already acknowledged and familiar values, he or she is not prepared to scrutinize new metaphors for their capacity to transform the commonplace. A poet will be celebrated only by a few, by his or her peers, or by the segment of the public that has retained the ability to contrast evaluatively the old and the new.

The life of the mind is the vast territory *between* the normal and revolutionary, familiar and unfamiliar, between living and dead metaphors. To concentrate on the extreme points of the continuum is to underestimate the concreteness and the importance of the middle territory. Neither the familiar use of ordinary language nor the delight caused by new metaphors deserves our exclusive attention. Of course, the creative play of genius, trying to produce the absolutely new, is justifiably the focus of fascination for those who combat "the anxiety of influence." But it is unlikely that a creative person is indifferent to whether his or her inventions will or will not become candidates for inclusion in the repertory of meaningful entities—verbal, mathematical, musical. Although for a while one will be content to contemplate alone "beauty bare," one will also entertain the hope that it will eventually be appreciated by others as well.

When someone introduces a new metaphor, or redescribes his or her experiences in an unfamiliar way, that redescription may attract the attention of others because it calls attention to something that is at least peripherally or subliminally relevant to their experience. In such encounters, solidarity with others may be enlarged. One who introduces a new metaphor reminds his or her hearers that a creative, nonroutine response to experience is possible. If the metaphor is felicitous, capable of echoing in someone else's experience, the hearer may discover a trace of solidarity with the creator of the metaphor. This is the way in which one's individual resources are supplemented by the inner resources of others.

New metaphors, according to the Davidson-Rorty view, are not governed by antecedent criteria of meaning. They start to acquire a meaning, however, if and when they begin to echo in other people's experiences. The emergence of such a common response may even signal the birth of a new criterion resulting from a meta-phor's "catching on." The new metaphor enters into a relation with already familiar meanings, causing them to shift in different, unex-pected directions. This shift is likely to involve a comparison with already familiar criteria to which the new metaphor becomes rele-vant. In addition, the inclusion of the new metaphor, which by then may be on the way to becoming a part of literal language, will signal an advance in understanding or coping with the phenomena in question. Compared to the previously used vocabulary, the new vo-cabulary *wins out.*

Comparison, however, means judgment, an evaluation about the worth or value of the suggested change. When the change is taken up into one's vocabulary, a segment of experience is rede-scribed, which may entail a change, even if a minor one, in the rede-scriber's self-image. He or she is now prepared to see the world via the recently altered, modified, or expanded vocabulary. Here the Kantian claim that the world and the self arise together gets an ex-panded application: The world and the self are modified together.

For any person anywhere the object of hope is twofold: to become exposed to worthwhile funded experience of the human race, beginning of course with what one's tradition has to offer, and to witness and to participate to some degree in the extension of that experience in new worthwhile directions. The furthest limit of this hope was expressed in the notoriously romantic desire of Goethe's Faust: "Whatever is allotted to the whole of mankind, that I wish to experience in my inner self, grasp with my mind the highest and deepest there is, heap upon my bosom all man's weal and woe, and thus extend my own self to be one with mankind, and like it, in the end meet shipwreck and perish." [13]

Faust's titanic ambition is of course overblown and unreal-istic; only a small fraction of this aspiration is realizable in anyone's life. Furthermore, each person's individual bents, capacities, and cir-cumstances circumscribe the scope and the character of values to be realized; not everything can be of interest to any one person. But one's hopes are likely to include events, activities, discoveries, and inventions that appear to have special significance, to meet impor-tant challenges, and to reach higher standards of excellence. The goodness of a person's life is conditioned by the realization of some of these hopes.

Hope and Liberal Democracy

If optimal human flourishing—personal and social—is, as we have seen, more likely to occur under the conditions of freedom and tolerance, then one object of hope is the spread of liberal democracies to all the peoples of the world. We have noted, however, that the presence of freedom in democratic states does not guarantee that human energies *will* be used optimally. If left to their own devices, people may choose, even legislate, practices that are not expressive of their best qualities. They may waste their lives on accumulating luxuries, or they may give themselves over to a pursuit of trivia, squandering their energies on unimportant matters, thus depleting resources needed for worthier projects and causes. They may acquire habits, such as drug abuse, that impair their health and diminish their ability to lead a decent life. Alternatively, while managing to stay within the limits of legality, they may abuse their economic wealth or political power to harm society by direct or subtle manipulation of their fellow citizens. Such activities will eventually put a strain on the viability of freedom and tolerance, thus threatening the liberal character of democracies in which such abuses are rampant.[14]

It is distortions like these that give rise to communitarian theories and movements. Rorty is aware of these objections. But in his opinion the liberal response to the communitarians' claim should be "that even if the typical character-types of liberal democracies *are* bland, calculating, petty and unheroic, the prevalence of such people may nevertheless be a reasonable price to pay for political freedom."[15] It is to be hoped, however, that such people will not become too prevalent, or that the harm done by them is minimized. But here, if the values of freedom and tolerance are indeed taken seriously, we have little more than hope, because, as Dostoyevsky shows in his legend of the Grand Inquisitor, an attempt to coerce people into goodness is fraught with dangers and not likely to succeed.

What a liberal democracy must rely on are the resources of

education, philanthropy, and political statesmanship. It must find ways to inspire its citizens to be both law-abiding and decent. Its devotees will also hope that the spiritual resources of the people will be spent not only on upholding political honesty, civic responsibility, and goodwill but also on encouraging high cultural and artistic achievements. Hence, liberal society will not limit itself to mere hoping but, through its leadership, will encourage in its rank and file not only profit motives (which can easily deteriorate into egregious greed) but also attitudes of public-spiritedness and respect for humane aspirations.

Education is the frontier of democracy. One of its tasks is to keep alive the idea that freedom makes room for self-making. Freedom is important because its absence translates into the presence of additional constraints on the effort to define oneself. Similarly, the absence of tolerance exposes the struggling individual to the interdictive powers of others. As an ally of political democracy, education can portray it as an experiment allowing human beings to choose forms of life that would result in the highest degree of individual and social flourishing and fulfillment. One of the lessons to be learned is that the social and political arrangements and institutions of liberal democracies are not inevitable. They are not enshrined in some antecedent reality of a theological, ontological, or biological sort. There are no forces working on behalf of democracy except those embodied in the efforts of individuals and groups who understand its relevance to what is worth hoping for.

The likelihood that political liberalism will succeed in affecting human practices globally is also a contingent matter, and to a large degree a matter of hope. As we have noted, those who accept the tenets of liberalism cannot justify them by appeal to some overarching truth. Justification here must take the form of apologetics, by showing the contrast between adopting these tenets and embracing some other alternative. The comparison cannot avoid being "invidious," that is, proceeding from an antecedent commitment to political liberalism as *better* than its alternatives.

If arguments can be offered for liberal democracy, they will take the form of comparison or analogy. To say, for instance, that logical forms of inference are valid is to point out that the failure to accept them prevents one from offering an argument at all. To have

66

any beliefs, one must be committed to accepting the logical consequences of these beliefs. Thus, the dispute of proponents of tolerance with its opponents turns on the acceptability of either practice. If the consequences of accepting intolerance as a general practice entail the prevention of human beings from coping successfully with their circumstances and reduce their chances of developing competence, self-confidence, and self-fulfillment, then intolerance *is* shown to be undesirable. The determining factor here is a commitment to human flourishing, and the seriousness of that commitment translates into willingness to *act* on its behalf. In this sense, such commitment can be unflinching. This is the point where one can say, "My spade is turned," and where justification cannot go further than saying, "This is what *we* do." To add that here "we" is equivalent to "democratic liberals" is a tautology. One's hope for humanity must be that at least some such "last ditch" justification will be acceptable.

From such reflective pragmatic acceptances there may emerge solidarity, a spirit of voluntary cooperation for the sake of individual and social well-being. Participation in such cooperative experiments can provide a convincing answer to the question "What ought I to do?" because through participation the place of humanity in the scheme of things is defined. In that sense, human beings *are* responsible for one another, not in the name of an already determined set of goals and purposes laid down in the essence of human nature, but in the sense of *giving* that nature a particular expression, within the context of possibilities presented by the historical situation. A solidarity emerging out of such an involvement is therefore not discovered but made, a work of minds, hearts, and hands that leave their imprint on their time, thus answering perhaps to some hopes of predecessors and possibly setting precedents for the following generation of human beings who will face the inescapable task of further self-definition.

The Present Prospects of Democracy

Hope is indispensable for coping. To cope is to move through the world knowingly and effectively; it is to be on the lookout for how it might be changed for the better. Since the objects of coping are our present circumstances, we cannot avoid discussing the historical situation in which we live (or into which, as Heidegger would put it, we are thrown). Such a discussion cannot stay on a general, abstract level if it is to contribute to our efforts to understand the background against which we are doing our thinking, even if that thinking begins with philosophical considerations. To say anything useful on the topic, philosophers as all-purpose intellectuals are still participants in a multidimensional activity, the parameters of which cannot be restricted in a way that would disallow referring to the actual social and political scene. To be at all helpful we need to use language that is closer to a journalistic analysis and commentary than to a style usually encountered in a philosophical text. Recall Rorty's observation that there is nothing sacrosanct about the boundaries between disciplines and genres. If coping involves becoming more familiar with our dangers and opportunities, we must not shy away from taking some liberties with conventional expectations in order to make thought relevant to life. The remainder of this chapter, threrefore, will cross the boundaries between political philosophy and politics, and between analysis and speculation, in the hope that such crossings will help us cope with the present situation.

The inescapability of the need for the intellectuals to talk about concrete contemporary issues became evident to Rorty when, challenged by Richard Bernstein's criticism of the bearing of his philosophical views on liberal democracy, he found himself forced to spell out his political credo. The ensuing debate made it clear that a useful philosophical reflection must step down from an ahistorical pedestal and work with historically relevant concerns. Such an engagement with practical problems on the part of philosophers would clearly please John Dewey, whose writings emphasized social activism and reconstruction. According to Dewey, problems of philosophers are problems of *people*. Accepting historicism, philosophy needs to speak to its times, in terms of actually existing preoccupations.

Bernstein sees problems with Rorty's defense of the Peircean view that one must start from beliefs one actually holds; he thinks that such a view encourages political conservatism. He in fact charges Rorty with supporting neoconservative views, and specifically with accepting the economic status quo and recommending cold war policies toward the Soviet Union, perceived as the chief enemy of liberal democracies. In Bernstein's view, Rorty on the one hand advocates a type of "aestheticized pragmatism" that has nothing to do with the philosophically serious social activism of Dewey but instead encourages an endless talk of "new tolerant *jouissance* of multiple language games and vocabularies,"[16] and on the other hand, in virtue of taking this philosophical line, provides "an ideological *apologia* for an old-fashioned version of cold war liberalism dressed up in fashionable 'post-modern' discourse."

Some of Bernstein's animus comes from his sympathies for the projects of philosophers like Habermas who still believe that democratic liberalism can be strengthened by providing for it a universal theoretical framework, such as that outlined in Habermas's *A Theory of Communicative Action*. Rorty has been critical of such hopes, believing that for public purposes "the relevant procedures are those of our historical situation" without needing some sort of universal import.[17] Similarly, he finds liberalism not helped by the Marxist terminology employed by some radicals. The radicals, in Rorty's opinion, still believe that Marxist terminology can be useful in unmasking bourgeois ideology and showing up its shortcomings. He thinks that this expectation is not likely to be fulfilled. Radicals are ineffective because they have become overly theoretical and are unable to provide any positive suggestions toward removing the evils they perceive in the capitalist system. Having given up any hope of controlling and containing such evils from within the system, they limit themselves to unmasking that system's imperialistic practices, at the same time minimizing the dangers of Soviet imperialism.[18]

More centrally, Rorty thinks that the radicals are mistaken in believing that decisions in the Kremlin are based on ideological convictions and that the debate with the Soviet hierarchy can be conducted on the level of theory. For many decades the real motivation of Soviet leaders has been the desire to maintain and expand their military and political power—the motivation of thugs rather than of theorists. What worries Rorty is that if Russian-style communism were to prevail, such key democratic institutions as freedom of the press, an independent judiciary, and autonomous universities would cease to exist. If communist expansionism were to continue, it would constitute a real threat to Western democracies. "Such fragile, flawed institutions, the creation of the last three hundred years, are humanity's most precious achievements. .... *Nothing* is more important than the preservation of these liberal institutions." [19]

In Rorty's opinion, Western democracies should not ignore the fact that the Soviet Union was a powerful and dangerous enemy of freedom, and that the danger may still persist. To Bernstein that position looks like advocacy of cold war. But Rorty is not uncritical of American external and domestic policies. As the leading power among affluent capitalist states (a collection he dubs the First World, distinguishing it from the communist Second World), the United States, like its allies, is notably selfish, greedy, and shortsighted. The political right within the First World, showing no interest in fostering equality, has put brakes on social democratic reforms designed along increasingly egalitarian lines and points to the need to contain communism as at least a partial justification for its policy.

As Rorty sees it, the hopes of liberal democrats to see the world moving in the direction of greater freedom, equality, and justice could be undermined from both sides: the external threat of imperialistic communism and the internal selfish and shortsighted pursuits of local oligarchs. Neither danger can be removed by devising more *Ideologiekritik,* more theoretical schemes; they are irrelevant to current political decisions, either in the East or in the West. But should the threat of totalitarian communism be defused, a democratic solidarity along the lines of a Rawlsian "overlapping consensus," concretely empirical and specific, could make the prospects of peace more likely. In the building of peace there is, of course, room for philosophical utopias and theoretical projections; in the long run some of them, when combined with the contributions of all-purpose intellectuals, novelists, and poets, are likely to affect political thinking. But such long-range influences, filtered through the private self-images of those who exert them, cannot take the place of more immediate policy decisions. The former can wait, the latter cannot, if the dangers are as real as they seem.

Political Contingencies

In projecting our fears and hopes into the future, we must always keep an eye on new, unforeseen contingencies. The West, for instance, still does not quite know what to make of the Gorbachev phenomenon and its likely development. It has been prepared by the ferment in the Communist world before Gorbachev emerged as the Soviet leader—the revisionism in Yugoslavia, radical changes in China, semirevolutionary transformations in Hungary and in Poland, and even the largely theoretical models of Eurocommunism. But no one could predict that the metaphors of *glasnost* and *perestroika* would introduce some real movement into the encrusted monolithic ideology of the Lenin-Stalin-Brezhnev type. Just what course the Soviet Union will take under and after Gorbachev no one can be certain. But there is at least a glimmer of hope that a degree of liberalization and democratization within the chief bulwark of communism may well keep increasing, eventually leading to a situation in which Western-style democracies need not feel threatened.

The apparently sincere desire on the part of both superpowers to embark on the process of dismantling at least some of the awesome nuclear arsenal has already introduced a sense of relief, although the world is far from being assured that some future contingencies will not reignite the nuclear race. Some fear that the relative relaxation in the Soviet Union, with the concomitant improvement of her economy, will in time make her more dangerous to Western democracies. On the other hand, there is also hope that a less oppressed and more prosperous Soviet population will be reluctant to support dangerous expansionist ventures.

One promising phenomenon is that under Gorbachev's leadership there is at least a willingness to describe the relationship between ideological opponents in a modified vocabulary. After decades of being warded off and rebuffed by stereotypical slogans mouthed by Soviet leaders, Western statesmen began to say that here is a communist statesman with whom they can talk business. Why is this so? Primarily because Gorbachev has abandoned the hitherto mandatory language of rigid Marxism-Leninism when talking about issues with representatives of noncommunist countries. Instead of formulaic responses expected and inevitably forthcoming from such spokesmen as Gromyko, Western leaders began to hear language that seems straightforward and businesslike.

This change is particularly evident on the question of nuclear disarmament. In talking about that issue Gorbachev has put the discussion on a level at which common human concerns, not divi-

sive political considerations, are dominant. In his public pronouncements he proclaims the conviction that a nuclear war would be a
disaster not only for a particular side but for everyone. In appealing
to the goal of mutual survival and peace, he has acknowledged the
need for Marxists and non-Marxists alike to agree on the moral desirability of eliminating the nuclear danger for everybody. In an article addressed "To the American Reader," he says that "it is quite
unnecessary for everyone to abandon his own faith and to adopt one
that is alien to him. Let each live by his own convictions and worship
his own God. We must calmly sum up the collective experience of
humankind and draw objective conclusions from objective prem-
ises." [20]

It is hard to disagree with his conclusion that "peace and life
are inseparably linked. Only on conditions of peace can people take
part in heated discussion about rights and freedoms, preferences
and biases." [21] Statements like these generate the hope that conversations between leaders representing different political systems can
be conducted in a vocabulary that makes agreements possible and,
more specifically, agreements concerning policies and actions that
threaten peace. That a resort to such a common vocabulary actually
takes place is encouraging. It shows that there are at least some areas
in which the language of Marxism is irrelevant. This change in itself
punctures the universalistic pretense of Marxist vocabulary to provide an all-encompassing description of what humanity can know
and hope for. To acknowledge that non-Marxists can be moved by
decent motives is to admit that one does not have to be a Marxist to
respect truth and morality.

The possibility of agreeing on at least some common good,
even such a fundamental sort as mutual survival, does not necessarily mean that the expansionist ambitions of Soviet communism are
renounced forever. One should not forget that as long as the Communist party continues to have a monolithic control over the affairs
of the people, its leaders will function as the party's mouthpieces.
Only when the power of the government is diffused among the
people through democratic mechanisms of representation will the
anxiety about potential ideological ambitions of the party subside.
The world's hope for peace is therefore conditioned by the contin-

ued process of democratization in the Soviet Union both under Gorbachev and his successors.

Perhaps a further liberalization of Soviet society is the result of a realization that its internal and external difficulties stem from an inadequate, outdated, and irrelevant vocabulary. One of the functions of that vocabulary was to *maintain* a barrier between the Marxist and non-Marxist worlds and to insist that only communism can provide a rational social order. So when Gorbachev asks the Westerners, "Why cannot the Soviet Union be trusted? What is the basis for such a mistrust?"[22] he can be reminded that his party, supposedly in the name of the high Marxist vision, did not hesitate, under Lenin's and Stalin's supervision, to destroy millions of innocent human lives.

This dark past of the Soviet state still worries liberal democracies. Can one rule out the possibility that totalitarian practices of the ruling party will not return? Cognizant of such contingencies, liberal democracies are reluctant to give control over people's lives to their governments on anything other than a temporary basis. This is a hard-won lesson of the past. To guard themselves against the contingency that the circles temporarily in power will seize power permanently, as the Communist party has done in the Soviet Union, democracies insist on periodic open elections through which the "rascals" can be thrown out and an entirely new batch of officials can be put in. Furthermore, in a democratic government the executive branch is limited by the legislature, scrutinized by the free press, and accountable to the courts. The wisdom of all these provisions and constraints does not need any "grounding" in "essential human nature" or in some metaphysical accounts of history; it is reconfirmed by observing the daily miseries inflicted on citizens when the state becomes totalitarian.

The understandably welcome "openness" recently proclaimed in the Soviet Union is being watched with wary eyes because the memory of totalitarian abuses is still fresh. In spite of that, the partial democratization of life—on economic, social, and cultural levels—is something that every freedom-loving person will applaud. If it is Gorbachev's wish to make it last and grow, then he will be perceived as a hero in the West as well. One can only applaud him when he says to the American reader: "There is no reason why anyone should assume the role of an omniscient, implacable oracle. There is no state that has nothing to learn from others. We are all teachers and pupils in one way or another."[23] One implication is that *Marxism* does not have the status of the omniscient, implacable oracle based on a discovery of a universal truth.

The changes going on in the Soviet Union under the leadership of Gorbachev do encourage a degree of hope. Even though for the greatest part of its existence the Soviet Union was governed by thugs, that is, leaders whose main method was the use of power camouflaged as ideology, it is an open question whether it *has* to remain so. Gorbachev *may* surprise us all, as Rorty wishfully speculates. The hope that he is moving away from autocratic totalitarianism may be signaled by his partial willingness to switch his vocabulary in the direction of distinctions characterizing liberal democracies. His attempts to introduce some openness into Soviet society and to loosen its social and economic structure are still too tentative to arouse confidence that they will really lead to real democratization; as the 1989 events in China demonstrated, they could be suddenly terminated by the entrenched class of party bureaucrats afraid to lose their prerogatives.

The big question for the First World countries is how to contribute to the movement away from the familiar aggressive stance of communist hardliners and toward a more accommodating, cooperative one. One thing is sure: A refusal to enlarge the area of dialogue and persuasion will leave the field to confrontation alone. But this option is foolish, if not suicidal, especially at the time when those who wield power are armed with awesome nuclear weapons. In the light of *that* contingency, of seeing not only the antagonists but possibly the rest of the world destroyed in a nuclear holocaust, it would be criminal to perpetuate the cold war, because it may become hot at any moment, given the presence of numerous tinderboxes all over the globe, especially in the Middle East.

In the light of these somber contingencies, Gorbachev's initiatives to defuse threatening situations and to encourage trust between the East and West are to be welcomed. It is good to see him acknowledge that "we share a common destiny and have to learn to be civilized neighbors on our planet"[24] and to admit that "we and the Americans bear the greatest responsibility toward the world's nations. Our two countries and peoples bear a special, unique responsibility to all human civilization." [25] If he expresses these commitments honestly and sincerely, in the "original meanings of these words," as he puts it,[26] then it would be a great error not to join him in this attempt to make the world safer and more decent.

If there ever was a time for serious diplomacy and for opening up channels of communication, of government to government and people to people, that time is now. But as Rorty notes in his political credo, the attempt at persuading potential aggressors to become less intransigent and more reasonable needs to be coupled with real efforts on the part of the First World to combat its own absorption in shortsighted, greedy, corrupt practices. Rorty is right in saying that liberal democrats have to fight on two fronts at once. They should not dismiss the thought that Communism will no longer threaten liberal democracies, but neither should they close their eyes to practices and policies inside their own countries that are shortsighted in foreign policy and callous about their own poor and disadvantaged. To the extent that these policies also affect the Third World nations, they will help decide whether these nations will opt for liberal or totalitarian systems. The latter alternative is less likely to be followed if the Third World has good reason to think that the leaders of the First World can be trusted and that they are truly effective in helping to solve their problems humanely.

America in the World

As the relationship of nations to one another can change as the result of some contingencies, such as the unexpected initiatives coming from the new leaders of the Soviet Union, so changes within a nation are triggered by unforeseen developments. Although in retrospect these developments may look perfectly understandable, even inevitable, it usually takes some time to discern their implications for the future. These implications sometimes require a shift in expectations and call for a redescription of objectives which may reveal new opportunities. Since such opportunities remain hidden unless and until the redescription is attempted, it is necessary to look at the changing situation in a new way.

The areas to be looked at may be quite mundane and at first

glance secondary. But when examined further, they disclose connections with other phenomena, thus contributing to a change in the entire *Gestalt* of the social, economic, and political situation. There is, for instance, one economic phenomenon in the world that is likely to have larger consequences, although at first it may appear self-contained and peripheral. Because of the spread of knowledge, technology, communication, and affirmative action, the pool of skilled workers in the world has increased dramatically. Goods that used to be produced by a few industrialized countries are now being manufactured all over the globe. A clear indication of this trend is the American trade imbalance. In addition to goods produced by other industrialized countries, for example, cars produced in Europe and in Japan, and raw materials such as oil, the United States buys a multitude of products made in Third World countries—Taiwan, Korea, India, Mexico, and many others. Even cars, for example, are now being imported from such recently industrialized countries as Korea and Yugoslavia.

Undoubtedly, the whole economic picture of global trade is complex and involves reciprocal transactions, including allocation of capital and of manufacturing facilities, but the simple fact is that the United States consumes much more than it produces, as is evident from the huge trade imbalance, in 1986 amounting to over $250 billion. What this means is that Americans now live on credit, extended by producing countries. True, the trade imbalance in part results from the restrictive policies of the trading partners, and if they were removed, markets would be open for many items produced in the United States. But the plain truth is that the United States is no longer the only supplier of goods that only a few decades ago were being produced nowhere else. The expectation is, of course, that American production will shift to high technology and will retain dominance as the key supplier of sophisticated goods, but increasingly these technological feats are being matched or even surpassed by other countries.

The present prosperity and affluence of Americans is subsidized by credits from abroad. At the same time, the promotion of affluent life-styles, of never-ending conspicuous consumption, is fueled by relentless advertising machinery. It is increasingly difficult, however, to maintain wealth differentials if an ever greater proportion of income has to be shared with those who actually produce the goods. The rise in the standard of living in the rest of the world is bound to diminish resources available to any one segment of it. It is unlikely that the spending level of Americans can go up indefinitely, with creditors abroad demanding a greater share in the form of higher prices for labor and products, in addition to interest on credit extended. After a while the perception of differentials translates into policies, and the time may come when the creditors will want to call in some debts. This likelihood is one reason for the rising level of anxiety among politicians and bankers about American trade deficits and the national budget imbalance.

That economic discrepancies involve explanations partly formulated in moral and political vocabulary, often invoking the language of fairness and justice, points up the connection of economic considerations with other, more general aspects of public and private life. Complex philosophical and moral adjustments may be necessary to acknowledge the hard fact that a growing equalization of economic activities in the world calls for a decrease of imbalance in degrees of prosperity. To describe such changes, one may have to begin with describing oneself, one's self-image and objectives, in a vocabulary so far avoided. One might say, for instance, that for the sake of global peace, fairness, and harmony, it is necessary to reduce one's aspirations for an inordinately high standard of living, compared with that available to the rest of the world's populations.[27] With such general objectives becoming a serious factor in one's thinking, one may find it morally questionable to keep promoting and intensifying an ethos of opulence, something which the domestic marketing and advertising machinery of American business seems to take for granted. In the light of the high visibility of poverty, misery, and suffering in many parts of the world, it may occur to some that to promote a glittering but wasteful style of living is morally wrong. Obsession with possessing more and more things and with heedless pursuit of proliferating pleasures is an offense against those who barely manage to survive. Such an obsession may also be perceived as the main cause of flouting obvious standards of ethical behavior, glaringly illustrated in scandals on Wall Street, in the relentless and unethical pursuit of profits, sometimes camouflaged as good business or even patriotism.

For the sake of survival and world peace, a shift of ethos may be required, away from materialistic preoccupations and from narrow concentration on one's own affairs, toward a more inclusive awareness of what is going on outside American borders. In compensation the willingness to lower the material standard of living will be rewarded by the consciousness that one is taking part in the effort to lift fellow human beings up from painful and demeaning marginal existences. One will begin to realize that in the shrinking global village self-involved provincialism is deplorable. Americans are often accused of dismaying ignorance about other nations and cultures and of appalling incuriosity about the pain suffered by human beings in other parts of the world. Not only Americans but also affluent citizens of other First World countries may find it morally desirable to tone down their headlong pursuit of "private bliss," to curb their tendency to privatize national experience, and to move toward a degree of democratic solidarity with other nations.

Such a shift in self-image, should it occur, would open up other opportunities, mobilizing many different resources. Instead of looking at desirable changes as remote and relegated to an indefinite future, one may begin to see them as requiring immediate attention. One will not limit oneself to educating the coming generation in the spirit of eventual reform but will also see the need to speak to the present political, economic, and cultural leadership. The new territory for moral action may be seen as a fertile ground by novelists, who, in the manner of Dickens, could dramatize both the social and the political consequences of the ingrained incuriosity about the suffering that afflicts great masses of humanity and the positive changes that would occur as the result of changing perceptions. Such perceptions might take the form of utopian visions of the kind of world our children and grandchildren might inhabit *if* we manage to create arrangements under which democratic solidarity can grow and flourish.

Starting with the Present

To view humanity as a changing and developing form of life is to be especially attentive to pragmatic options thrown onto our path by actual contingencies and opportunities. Such a pragmatism is humanistic not in the sense of trying to bring about something already defined, an essential human nature, but in the sense of *creating* something better than what we have known before. Since there is no blueprint of how this could be done, this kind of pragmatism is not committed to a method and is not capturable in terms of a universal theory. By now the human experiment has gone on long enough for us to learn that history is never fully controllable and keeps throwing out unforeseen challenges.

One of the unexpected but acutely felt consequences of increasing technological control over nature is the population explosion. Increasingly, it invades our consciousness. A more abundant food supply and more effective medical know-how made it possible for greater numbers of human groups to survive and multiply. As a result, the planet's ecological resources are being stretched to meet ever-growing demands. This fact poses challenges for societies to find ways of coping with constantly increasing scarcities, which inescapably involve us in moral issues: how to deal with situations that cause hunger, pain, and other deprivations.

Speaking concretely, how are the people inhabiting the affluent First World and the relatively well off Second World to react to pitiful pictures of starving children shown on television screens? Such spectacles are difficult to ignore, for, because of instant communication, they confront us with the *present* and *actual* miseries of fellow human beings, not some second- or thirdhand descriptions of what is already safely in the past. In addition, we know that help *could* be on the way without delay, in the form of plentiful stocks of grain that could be airlifted to those who suffer. Under such circumstances it is much harder to declare oneself absolved of responsibility because of practical inability to help. We know that in this case, "We ought because we can." So if we choose not to act, we cannot quite dismiss the suspicion that something is morally amiss with us, which is likely to affect our self-image. It would be disingenuous here to hide behind the doctrine of human nature; such a move would self-deceivingly absolve us of guilt or conveniently explain away our indifference and inaction.

It is similarly disingenuous to acquiesce morally in the suffering caused by the violence against others perpetrated in the head-long pursuit of nationalistic, ideological, or religious goals. It is no excuse to point out truistically that such pursuits have been with us ever since human beings began to fight for survival—against other forms of life and against destructive forces of nature—by banding together into tribes and hordes. No normative claims are implied by the observation that for millennia humanity lived without any moral qualms about promoting one's own at the experse or even elimination of the neighbor or the foreigner. Such behavior was considered an unavoidable aspect of human nature. But it *is* open to us today to question this picture of ourselves. Such questioning is, after all, the injunction of world religions that already for centuries have not found it unrealistic to preach love and goodwill toward strangers, and even the unity of all humankind.

That successes have been scored in this endeavor, history is a witness. Contradicting the Hobbesian account of the state of nature, nonaggression pacts have been signed, and good-neighbor policies have been proclaimed and followed. Alliances and organizations have been formed and have often succeeded in putting an end to particular wars and conquests. In proclamations at least, aggression is universally condemned today. Nevertheless, nationalistic, ethnic, and religious alliances continue to invoke exclusionary interests as justifying violence against neighbors. When threats loom, the principle of self-determination and self-defense is reasserted, precluding the growth of solidarity with other human beings. That principle is usually invoked to escape the charge of wickedness and immorality; the blame can be put on the allegedly aggressive behavior of others. Given the long and complicated history of relations between neighboring states, there is no shortage of grievances and complaints to which one can resort in order to "justify" one's own aggression.

But in regard to massive suffering resulting from hunger and deprivation, the infliction of pain on others by waging nationalistic, ideological, and religious wars is more and more visible to the rest of the world. As the callousness and incuriosity about starving people are harder and harder to hide, so the inhumanity to other human beings—in killing fields or internment camps—is more and more visible to more and more people through the efficiency of global mass media. The outrage against Hitler's extermination camps did not break out as long as they were kept secret, as long as they were not visible. But as the scale and the specific horrors of this crime were brought before the eyes of humanity, revulsion became a potent moral force. "Never again!" became the obviously moral resolve.

A similar, even if diluted and belated, reaction was registered to the disclosures about Stalin's Gulag Archipelago. The present Soviet leadership cannot quite ignore these disclosures and is pledging itself to the prevention of such horrible abuses, even if the abuses are still disingenuously attributed to the "personality cult" of an aberrant leader. So it is dismaying and dispiriting to watch the continuation of brutality going on today unabated in many parts of the world and, besides battleground slaughter, taking the form of terrorism and indiscriminate reprisals—killing civilians, women, and children, and brutally attacking innocent bystanders. The persistence of bloody violence keeps reviving the suspicion that aggression is indeed innate.

But here again it is defeatist to seek refuge in a global theory of human nature, this time pessimistically defined. The acceptance of such a theory shifts attention away from the contingent conditions that give rise to violence. The prime challenge to contemporary humanity is to identify and to cope with these conditions. It can be a challenge only if one refuses to regard acquiescence in aggressive reactions as inevitable, an unchangeable fact of human nature. Such a refusal will direct attention to special contexts in which resort to violence occurs. Just as recognition of the unprecedented dangers inherent in nuclear warfare appears to be at least partly successful in curbing hostility between the superpowers, so the recognition of the potential consequences of murderous feuding among nations may contribute to finding peaceful ways.

The situation is aggravated by the fact that among the consequences is the possibility that armed conflict among powers now thought to be without nuclear weapons will eventually involve the use of nuclear weapons. For instance, since the continued availability of Middle Eastern oil is of vital interest to members of the First World, it would be extremely dangerous for world peace for the United States and the Soviet Union to confront each other in the context of some future local war. Moreover, the monopoly on nuclear arms is eroding. It is widely assumed that Israel has nuclear capability and that Pakistan and India are secretly trying to achieve it. What if any of these nations, seeing itself in a desperate situation, were to resolve to use nuclear weapons? Would it be possible to prevent a more extensive nuclear exchange?

Besides the military and political considerations affecting world peace there are also economic consequences to take into account. Some countries in hostile postures toward one another require huge military investments that create long-term depletion of material resources that could otherwise be spent on food and ecological preservation. Some of these countries are blind to the tragic waste of resources so urgently needed to keep life going at a decent level of well-being; they are blind to the suffering caused by an unbalanced emphasis on military spending. The first step toward a more responsible stance would be for those in positions of power and influence to become aware of the consequences of their incuriosity about the likely concomitants of belligerent and destructive policies.

Hope is nourished when fresh options are perceived, when conflicts are solved by mutual accommodation, and when dangers are transformed into opportunities. Such transitions require new metaphors, a new vocabulary in which people can redescribe themselves. But a redescription can take place only against the background of presently prevailing circumstances, which must be realistically and soberly appraised. Project making must begin with stocktaking. In the search for new answers it may be wise to examine previous attempts to deal with similar situations. Among such attempts is, for example, the proposal to work toward some kind of world order under a common government. This idea ran aground on the issue of national sovereignty, exacerbated by sharp ideological divisions. These obstacles still exist and are likely to prevent the revival of the idea of world government. But it is not to be assumed that the only alternatives are either status quo or some form of world order. Fresh thinking may be required. On the assumption that ideological rigidities both in the First World and the Second begin to soften (and there are signs that they might), one may work toward some other ways in which cooperative actions and policies can produce a more peaceful and harmonious world. Such policies need not be wholly original; they may tinker with mechanisms already in place. The United Nations organization would be a much more effective instrument if some of its structures were modified or re-formed. Many a war would not have taken place if the Security Council had dropped its veto provision, thus forcing potential belligerents to respect the collective desire for peaceful solutions to disagreements among nations.

It is a mistake to overlook and dismiss the contingencies of the imagination. It was the imagination displayed by particular leaders that loosened the anxious grip of the Communist parties on the peoples of the Second World. The successful defection of Yugoslavia from the Stalinist camp and the early protests and rebellions in Hungary, East Germany, and Czechoslovakia have planted the seeds from which eventually grew the movements of revision and reform. In the oldest and largest Communist establishments—the Soviet Union and China—the realization that reforms are imperative came more slowly and is to be attributed to the initiative of individuals who dared to question the rigid official dogma. Even if the pace of change is slow and unpredictable, not precluding setbacks and reversals, only a die-hard pessimist would refuse to entertain fresh hopes.

We need not view the changing global scene exclusively in terms of theories and formulas derived entirely from the knowledge of the past. For even that knowledge allows of redescriptions that put the present dangers and options in a new light.

There is no reason to subscribe to an "essentialist" view of history and to see the past as a solid monolithic set of inexorable facts. Like the present, the past is not accessible without a reconstruction and without interpretation. Indeed, if we remember that the past was in part made by human beings, by how they perceived and coped with *their* contingencies, we will have even less reason to think that *our* contingencies leave us no room to maneuver. That's not the way the present feels. It may not always feel, à la William James, "like a fight," but some of its components certainly engage our moral feelings and concerns, prompting our imaginations to exert themselves. There is much room for such exertion—by all thoughtful people, whether novelists, theorists, ironists, or intellectuals of any other stripe.

There *is* room for concrete, piecemeal proposals, and there is also room for utopian, synoptic, or holistic visions. There is more than meets the eye in Rorty's endorsement of William James's view that truth is that which is good in the way of belief. This view is an open invitation to contribute to the continuing effort to make sense of the human experiment on earth. The results of that experiment are not laid out in the Platonic heaven but are contingent on how we understand our situation and our options. Hope is an indispensable ingredient of that understanding.

CHAPTER FOUR

Hope and Philosophy

Rorty's Challenge

In a review Richard Bernstein describes Rorty's *Philosophy and the Mirror of Nature* as "one of the most important and challenging books to be published by an American philosopher in the past few decades."[1] That book (now translated into six languages) and Rorty's subsequent writings have stimulated a lively conversation not only among philosophers but among those in other disciplines as well. This is not surprising. Although Rorty considers his work as continuing and elaborating themes sounded by such people as Hegel, Nietzsche, Heidegger, James, Dewey, Wittgenstein, Gadamer, Habermas, Quine, Davidson, and Derrida, his crisply and eloquently stated views, sometimes putting an unexpected gloss on a familiar word—"edification" or "conversation," for example—have far-reaching implications. Because of that, his work has provoked a great deal of commentary, some of it critical.

One reason for the "Rorty industry" is his questioning the value of the epistemological emphasis in our central Plato-Descartes-Kant tradition. However, some critics find Rorty's account of that tradition not always accurate (with Daniel Dennett playfully estimating that accuracy at 0.742).[2] The criticisms turn on the importance of keeping some distinctions alive or on giving new interpretations to some crucial philosophical terms. There is also resistance to his view that language does not "correspond" to the world, that all knowledge is intralinguistic and does not need an extralinguistic foundation. The reasons for this resistance are spelled out by C. G. Prado in his book *The Limits of Pragmatism*. A highly sympathetic reader and interpreter of Rorty's writings, Prado nevertheless finds himself on the side of those who insist on some form of realism. He thinks that Donald Davidson is on the right track in believing that the question of how words hook on to the world is not idle. "The depth of Davidson's view is that he understands how, in spite of being limited to one end of the relation, we can say that the whole language does 'correspond' to the way things are."[3] Warranted assertability cannot displace truth. In order to escape the charge of relativism, we still need a theory of truth, without embracing either Platonic realism or Cartesian certainty. Prado concludes that Davidson's ongoing work toward such a theory is a viable philosophical enterprise; "a continued acceptance of realism as coherent is neither self-delusion nor a failure to understand the Rortyan critique."[4]

Prado sides with Davidson in thinking that "the world still determines truth, but without serving as a *relatum* in a correspondence relation that *makes* some sentences or beliefs true," thus getting "a kind of correspondence from holistically juxtaposing language and belief to the world—not a Kantian noumenal world, just the world."[5] Rorty is mistaken in claiming that nothing at all can be said about the world as a determinant of truth. By leaving room for a defense of philosophical realism, Prado, following Davidson, would thereby extend the reach of philosophy to extralinguistic matters. He also seems to agree with Caputo's claim that without such an extralinguistic reference, without some theoretical answer to the question of how words hook on to the world, Rorty "ends up with just talk."[6] Interestingly enough, Prado is prepared to say that only such a philosophical articulation of such a reference to the world enables us to get things *right* and to claim *correctness* for our descriptions. He also accepts Bernard Williams's arguments that natural science doesn't just give us another narrative about the world but produces "retrospective objectivity," thus allowing us to admit the possibility of cumulative convergence on the truth about the world.

What could Rorty say in response to these claims? For one thing, he does not deny that the world, nonphilosophically understood, stands in a causal relation to language; he only claims, as did Wittgenstein, that *that* relation cannot be described in language, because language cannot reach that far. A fortiori, we cannot produce *statements* about that relation which would be either right or correct. When Davidson says that in giving up the dualism of schema and content, "We do not give up the world, but reestablish touch with the familiar objects whose antics make our sentences and opinions true or false,"[7] his use of the word "antics" seems to acknowledge the sheer contingency of the causal relationship of the world to language; antics cannot be either right or correct—they simply give us the world.

As I have argued in chapter 1, the mistake of representationism or correspondism lies in thinking that in warranted assertions not the world itself is being presented but merely its surrogate, a shadow. As Wittgenstein observed, in using language correctly we proceed without (philosophical) justification but not without right.[8] That right is earned by learning language and does not need a *metaphysical* right to back it up. "Normal science" gives us all the objectivity we need; we accept its verdicts and do so for indefinite stretches of time without any qualms as long as we have no reason to think that the antics of the world are changing. I don't think that Rorty would disagree with Prado that "we can retrospectively discern progress of a real sort,"[9] and that there is a "cumulative growth of scientific knowledge,"[10] when by progress is meant the replacement of an old theory by a new one which clears up the difficulties of the old. Many of Prado's strictures against Rorty's position are less damaging than they appear. That he is aware of this is borne out by a statement on the last page of his book: "My feeling is that Rorty would dismiss the foregoing by admitting that we *do* capture how things are in our growing competence at coping with the world."[11]

Rorty's criticism of the epistemological bias is suspected of being an attack on the rational foundations not only of science but of morality and politics as well. Because he does regard it as important to discredit the quest for Nature's Own Language or the Essence of Human Nature, he returns to these themes again and again. His repeated injunctions against foundationalism, his dichotomizing arguments into ahistorical and ethnocentric, look almost obsessive to Richard Bernstein.[12] As we have already noted in the previous chap-

ter, Bernstein perceives in Rorty's lightheartedness about foundationalism a lack of seriousness about the philosophical enterprise.

In his book *Philosophy in Question* David R. Hiley places
Rorty's views in the tradition of Pyrrhonian skepticism, which calls
into question the Platonic conception of philosophy in order to
bring about a tranquil and untroubled acceptance of the contingency
of traditions and the fallibility of common life. Hiley claims that
some readers of Rorty's writings find in them "a kind of metaphilosophy of boredom that allows for an end of philosophy in the sense
of its termination and that justifies a withdrawal, not to some position anterior to metaphysics as in Heidegger, but to a position where
one simply refuses to be involved in the philosophical conversation."[13] Another conclusion is that Rorty "seeks to trivialize philosophy and its place in culture in order that we can quit doing philosophy whenever we like."[14]

Bernstein discerns a lack of seriousness also in Rorty's skepticism that the tasks of reconstructing society call for finding a general method. Bernstein cites Dewey's observation that the gulf between the actual and the possible cannot be bridged by piecemeal
policies undertaken ad hoc.[15] Like Dewey, he would preserve the
role of philosophy as reconstructive agent of society. He chides Rorty
for limiting himself to offering examples, without providing arguments to resolve conflicts, especially since the historical consensus
of our tradition, as Alasdair MacIntyre has pointed out,[16] is far from
being solid, harmonious, or coherent. According to Bernstein, even
if the principles of liberal democracy do not have ahistorical support, they can be justified in other ways. By justification one may
mean what John Rawls meant by it, namely, "a matter of the mutual
support by many considerations, of everything fitting together into
one coherent view."[17]

Rorty's reluctance to look for some theoretical devices for
restructuring society and his willingness to settle for hermeneutics
viewed not as a method but an ad hoc "muddling through"[18] look to
Bernstein as evidence of irresponsible lightheartedness. He is worried that such an attitude is likely to result in pernicious relativism.
Already in his review of *Philosophy and the Mirror of Nature* he
asked: "What are the social practices to which we should appeal?

How do we discriminate the better from the worse?"[19] A similar concern is voiced by John Dunn:

> Since the question of whether an existing assemblage of human practices is essentially appropriate as it stands or whether it requires drastic and systematic reconstruction is at the core of social and political theory, a simple appeal to the authority of practice has no determinate content and is necessarily either evasive, invidious or vacuous.[20]

Another critic sees in Rorty's view a defense of a specific ideological project. According to Cornel West, "Rorty's neo-pragmatism is, in part, a self-conscious postphilosophical ideological project to promote the basic practices of bourgeois capitalist societies while discouraging philosophical defenses of them."[21] Like Bernstein, West accuses Rorty of offering no philosophical defense of his political position, but, unlike Bernstein, he is unwilling to label it "humanism," preferring to call it "a form of ethnocentric posthumanism." He is unhappy with Rorty for "refusing to push his own project toward cultural and political criticisms of the civilization he cherishes."[22] He finds Rorty "unmindful of the decline of liberalism,"[23] and possibly endorsing the existing order,[24] a charge similar to that made by Bernstein.

A further look at what bothers West shows, however, that he would not be happy with Bernstein's championing of methods recommended by Dewey. West's own priorities would move political conversation in directions he believes not to be sufficiently acknowledged in the dominant American culture, namely, the concerns of marginal peoples and such social phenomena as class exploitation, state repression, patriarchy, and racism. Unlike Bernstein, he includes Dewey in this criticism. "Dewey's libertarian democratic socialism and Rorty's revisionist liberalism view history through American lens."[25]

Interestingly enough, John R. Wallach is not concerned that the social and political conversation promoted by Rorty will encourage conservatism. But he is worried about the likely impact of edifying discourse, or more correctly, about the lack of it. He thinks that Rorty "would not assign a *privileged* status to prevailing conversations and traditions he likes—in fact, he praises unconventional views. They are the stuff of 'edifying' rather than 'systematic' or 'normalizing' discourse," that is, discourse of poets and verbal revolutionaries.[26] But such people, Wallach continues, tend "not to be taken seriously in the actual deliberations of citizens," with the consequence that "Rorty's perspective favors the rulers . . . rather than the citizens themselves."[27]

A related worry is expressed by Jeffrey Stout. Sympathetic to Rorty's views on liberal society, he nevertheless finds them giving the impression of smugness because they do not sufficiently acknowledge the force of communitarian misgivings. There ought to be, suggests Stout, "the mean between smug approval of the *status quo* and the wistful alienation from it—the mean between liberal apologetics and implicitly utopian criticisms."[28] Stout distrusts communitarians because the kind of solidarity *they* would encourage is likely to have "a disastrous totalizing effect on us."[29] Echoing views expressed by Gilbert Mailaender, Stout thinks that a liberal society ought not to limit itself to safeguarding the individual pursuit of private goals and projects but should also encourage citizens to "find *some part* of their identity as citizens of a republic directed to the common good."[30] Emphasis on private pursuits becomes a self-fulfilling prophecy, it "hides the actual extent of our commonality from view."[31]

Stout suspects that the actual effect of the language of individualism has been to treat social practices as merely "external goods," that is, as not possessing intrinsic value but as merely instrumental to private goals. Thus, for instance, even the intrinsic *telos* of caring for the sick is overwhelmed by goods and roles that are alien to it. So are other practices that become embodied and objectified in institutions—professional and athletic associations, business partnerships, and governmental agencies. Intrinsic values of social practices are lost sight of, and participation in them is treated as somehow detached from and irrelevant to private fulfillment. Stout believes that MacIntyre is right in arguing that the pursuit of material goods, power, and status loses moral content when it ignores the intrinsic positive role played by social practices and instead "externalizes" institutions which make that pursuit possible.

Stout expresses the hope that we will protect social prac-

tices as intrinsically valuable to liberal society and will not limit ourselves to "simply private bonds and the individual pursuit of external
goods."[32] Like Rorty, he thinks that this protection will need to pay
attention to "daily detail." As Dewey advocated, instead of looking for
general principles, we must deal with issues concretely, "by drawing
the line here and there in countless particular cases," that is, by cul-
tivating *phronesis.*[33] Modern *phronesis,* however, needs to pay attention to changing circumstances and therefore cannot limit itself to
following traditional roles and models. When Stout observes that the
creative task of every generation is moral *bricolage* and praises Jefferson and Martin Luther King for using eclectic moral language,[34]
he acknowledges that a mere revival of classical Aristotelian virtues
will not guarantee the moral health of society. To be of use at all,
these virtues need to be blended with the demands of the moment.

In spite of partial agreements, the critics' uneasiness about
Rorty's views stems primarily from their fear that "edifying" philosophy is either irrelevant to social and political concerns or encourages acquiescence in the status quo. This impression seems reinforced by Rorty's defense of the "thin" notion of the self, as being
nothing more than a web of beliefs and desires, articulated along the
Humean-Nietzschean-Sartrean lines. Hiley claims, for instance, that
such a view of the self is purely reactive and nonsubstantive.[35] In
contrast, Michael Sandel defends a "substantive" notion of the self as
a necessary condition for a viable community. Noting that Rorty
often appeals to our democratic or Christian ideals, Charles Guignon asserts that such ideals do not square with "pragmatist" or "hu-
manist" labels.[36]

How telling are these criticisms? Do they do serious damage
to Rorty's general position? It seems that to a large extent the critics'
fears are either unfounded or rest on a misunderstanding. First of
all, Rorty could counter Bernstein's complaint about "obsessive" concern with foundationalism by pointing out that it is precisely such
obsession with the idea of providing a universal underpinning for
all knowledge that has prevented philosophers from paying attention to other areas of legitimate intellectual and practical issues.
Being playful toward the fascinated fixation on ahistorical foundations is an effective way of being serious about historically and con-
tingently important matters. The philosophers' universalist preten-

sions and their fondness for epistemological/metaphysical methods are by and large being ignored by the rest of the culture. What professional philosophers discuss in their journals and books is not as influential a part of culture as they tend to think. Similarly, the suspicion that Rorty indulges in a kind of metaphysics of boredom is wide of the mark, if the target of boredom is not philosophy as such but the monotonous obsession with problems that privilege the scientistic and constructive side over the hermeneutic and reactive.

Likewise, the charge of trivialization rests on a misunderstanding. Rorty does use this word when he recommends that we "see both the coherence and correspondence theories as noncompeting trivialities," but this remark is to be understood as a part of his skepticism about whether anything really useful turns on devising a philosophical *theory* of truth, if such theories encourage us to look down upon a more humble and yet more inclusive and therefore more useful pragmatic notion of truth as that which, in William James's phrase, is "good in the way of belief." Rorty would like to have this use of "truth" preserved for conversation about all kinds of issues, and that's why he is inclined to relegate theories of truth to Philosophy. If we accept the distinction between philosophy and Philosophy, it would be incorrect to say that we can quit doing philosophy whenever we like. If by "philosophy" is meant Philosophy—an endeavor to "ground" current practices of justification in something ahistorical—then Rorty—like the Pyrrhonic skeptics, Montaigne, Rousseau, and Hume—*is* "disconnecting philosophy and the good life."[37] But his point is that life could be *improved* by such disconnection.

What is called a metaphilosophy of boredom may be just the discovery that the hunt for Nature's or Human Nature's Own Language is a delusion. To give up this hunt is to experience a sense of relief. The history of human thought can be seen not as converging on one Great Truth but as a series of attempts to devise good but optional ways of being human. When the aspirations of metaphysicians are seen in this light, they will be regarded not as revealing an ahistorical Secret but as providing alternative models for self-understanding and self-creation. It is this discovery, I believe, that prompts Rorty in describing our situation to make a more prominent use of the language of aesthetics, delight, and *jouissance*.

His advocacy of the reactive, edifying, and hermeneutic sort of philosophy is just a corollary of his criticism of philosophy dominated by the systematic construction of rules and criteria. He admits that the reactive side of philosophy is parasitic on the constructive one, which means that the latter can never be *replaced* by the former. But philosophy can be kept alive and progressive by making use of new vocabularies and fresh metaphors.

When urged to furnish guidelines for criticizing existing social practices, Rorty can reply that for that purpose *general* answers are of little use. To provide such answers would be once more to engage in a philosophical debate about the *essential* features of human needs and goals. This would take us back on the path Rorty has renounced as unprofitable; again we would be talking about essential human nature. He cheerfully admits that answers to *specific* questions would have to be invidious, that is, selected from the larger repertory of beliefs to which we subscribe, which at the time of considering the questions would not themselves appear questionable, and to which we subscribe unflinchingly. Such beliefs are not regarded as optional at the time they are held, although they are understood to be optional in the sense that were we to be born into some other culture or to undergo a conversion, they would lose their appeal.

We may recall that when challenged to give specific content to his democratic liberalism, Rorty did so by spelling out his "political credo," thus speaking to concrete concerns voiced by West as to the proper object of philosophical interest. Inasmuch as Rorty too would be in favor of policies that would speak to these concerns, he, like West, does not accept all of American culture as it is. But he would remind West that needed remedies and reforms must appeal to principles, institutions, and procedures already operative in the American democratic system; they must rely on persuasion rather than force, if the values of freedom and tolerance are to be preserved. Just how such conflicts and tensions in the American social fabric are to be resolved is the task of all concerned citizens, including intellectuals of all kinds—politicians, journalists, political theorists, and in some contexts even philosophers, the "all-purpose intellectuals."

Rorty's general reply to his critics could include a reminder that his *moral* objective in opposing exclusive commitment to ahistorical analysis was precisely the desire to make more room for the articulation of concrete human concerns at levels where people can appeal to the norms already at work in their society, in their day. What *other* norms are they to appeal to? It is not surprising, therefore, that his reply to Bernstein, who pressed him for more than just the criticism of ahistoricism, took the form of giving examples of what he would say when asked about the historico-political situation of our society. As we have seen, it differs from the way Cornel West perceives the situation, but certainly it is more specific than what Bernstein offers in his general endorsement of Dewey's call for social reconstruction.

Rorty's reluctance to view the human self as something more than a web of beliefs and desires has two sources, I believe. On the one hand, he is not convinced by the Platonic and Kantian arguments that to be a human being one must be in possession of some essential metaphysical core, call it soul or the *real* self. On the other hand, he suspects that when one regards the self as constituted by society, it is the historical, parochial values of a given society that will provide the "substance" of such a communal self. To say that a person is "constituted" by his or her beliefs and desires, can be, however, as "thick" as are these beliefs and desires, and these can be thick indeed and can be held unflinchingly. Rorty need not disagree with Stout's claim that society, through its institutions, including those of public opinion, is entitled to make claims on the allegiance of citizens. But he would be reluctant to regard the self as partly constituted by the community because it is possible for those who claim to speak for the community to pressure citizens into conformity against their better judgment and conscience. Stout himself warns that communitarianism tends to have a "totalizing" effect, and his misgivings have been sounded by others in our recent past. Herbert Marcuse, for instance, deplored the emergence of what he called "one-dimensional man."[38] Recognizing that the authority of the state expresses contingent and transitory values embraced by a particular community, Rorty would like to leave as much room as possible for the independent judgment of each citizen. There is little room for this, if any, in a totalitarian state. But even in a liberal democracy, as J. S. Mill noted, it is difficult to escape the tyranny of the majority, especially at a time like ours, when, with powerful electronic media at its disposal, the majority can "brainwash" its malleable citizens and consumers into enthusiastic, if blind, conformity.

A conscientious citizen will make this conformity depend on his or her considered judgment. Commitment to such judgments to that extent "congeals" or "crystallizes" one's web of beliefs. If this is what happens, then it is not the case that Rorty separates the question of autonomy from the question of personhood and community.[39] Autonomous participation is especially evident when the "reconstructive" process in a society is going on. At a time when a policy or a social practice is being scrutinized for its eligibility for continuance, acceptability, or modification, the person doing the scrutinizing speaks in the name of at least a potential community to which supporting or critical considerations would be acceptable. The set of beliefs which at the time of such restructuring or revolution are not questioned could be said to constitute the person's "substantive" self. To that limited extent, I believe, Rorty could agree with Sandel's notion of community as constitutive of the individual. But because the existential, reactive capacity of a person is not thereby abrogated, the beliefs and commitments of that person will still be experienced as optional, that is, not dictated by some essential human nature or the "real" self.

To say that criticism of one's culture can only be piecemeal—never "by reference to eternal standards"—is not to "eliminate a place for rational criticism of moral and social values."[40] What is to be kept in mind is that in a moral or political arena problems can be resolved only if the parties to the dispute treat each other as conversational *partners,* that is, persons interested in resolving the difference and arriving at consensus. As long as they rely on persuasion and not on trickery or force, a consensus, if reached, will be voluntary; it will not be "merely an exchange of attitudes toward our current condition."[41] Rorty's appeal to the "conversation of humankind" is not an updated emotivism.

With regard to the relationship of an individual to a community, Rorty would like to guard against the tendency on the part of human beings to exhibit a false sense of self-importance by claiming attachment to a more powerful whole, as symbolized by trendsetters, role models, and idols of the masses. Such a sense of self-importance is undeserved because it is unearned. It is not based on a genuine individual judgment and achievement but is primarily secondhand and all too often third-rate, merely mimicking the Manager, the Therapist, or the Rich Aesthete. While in affluent democratic societies such ersatz culture and politics may lack the horror of totalitarian manipulation and oppression, it nevertheless threatens a free development of genuinely individual tastes and values. All too readily it absorbs citizenry into a cultural framework with its "objective," external constraints, undermining the possibility of attaining a truly unforced consensus through a free interplay of edifying, hermeneutic explorations. Rorty believes that we need to make room for such creative explorations and therefore is reluctant to jump on the bandwagon of communitarianism, no matter how "traditional," "time-honored," and benign. His humanistic pragmatism is based on the view that humanity is still in the making and on the hope that a liberal society can protect the seeds of its optimal growth.

The Future of Philosophy

What hopes can we entertain for philosophy? Put this way, the question is ambiguous. It may mean: How will the subject fare in the future? Will it survive? If so, what shape will it take? Alternatively, it can mean: Will philosophy prove to be of use to society? If so, of what use? What contributions, if any, can we expect from it? Political considerations discussed at the end of the preceding chapter have a direct bearing on the question whether philosophy as a discipline will survive. Should future societies be governed by regimes that suppress the freedom of thought and speech and abolish free universities, philosophy as it is practiced in liberal democracies will disappear from the scene. This circumstance may not prevent some stubborn souls from thinking and putting their thoughts on paper (perhaps after a day spent grinding lenses), but institutionalized exchange and publication of philosophical views will be discouraged or replaced by political propaganda, as when *Voprosy Filosofii* in Stalin's day featured his articles as the latest and only truth about all aspects of reality.

Rorty is quite optimistic about the survival of philosophy under conditions of political freedom and relative economic affluence. He believes that "there is no danger of philosophy's 'coming to an end.'"[42] It is likely to fare well wherever people are not preoccupied with daily cares and where the society is affluent enough to afford and to support free universities. Indeed, as we have noted, he thinks that nothing is more important than safeguarding conditions under which such institutions are possible. Given the natural propensity to investigate and to reflect, people will continue to explore topics that for whatever reasons engage their attention. There is no way to predict the directions, style, and genres which this activity will take on. It is also likely that through an intense exchange in publications and conferences and through departmental appointments and promotions some particular fashions and fads will keep emerging as temporarily dominant, giving way to others once the interest and support are spent. It is worth noting that while Rorty himself became critical of the dominance of the epistemological/analytic mode in Anglo-American philosophy, he did not deny that this mode has its special virtues. For *its* purposes, the analytical style is *good,* he observed.[43] As long as there are people with interests and talents to pursue the kind of questions with which philosophical analysis is concerned, the analytical style will not disappear.

As to the shape that philosophy—if allowed to flourish—should take, the hopes voiced for it will express convictions developed within the pursuit itself. Rorty's hope is that more attention will be given to the reactive, edifying, or hermeneutic mode of philosophizing.[44] His critique of the epistemological mode is but an aspect of a campaign to reverse the order in which the components of coping have been traditionally presented. In his view, edifying philosophers "present themselves as doing something different from, and more important than, offering accurate representations of how things are."[45] The phrase "more important than" could be underscored in his text, because in the phenomenon of coping the dimensions of hope and action have a certain priority over the dimension of knowledge. Knowledge and its criteria are the *result* of a hopeful search for moves that would make us more effective in handling our environment, thus solving our problems and producing greater satisfactions and more delight. Although the reactive, edifying mode of philosophy always needs the background of the criterial and constructive rendering of experience, it pushes conversation in new directions and continues it along paths that deviate from those that have been followed so far. The rationale for treating the criterial approach only as a background for fresh thinking, for new metaphors and vocabularies, is that progress depends on introducing and exploring new perspectives.

Rorty believes that philosophical thinking can be revitalized if it is decoupled from the idea that thought must latch on to something preexistent, either theological or metaphysical in nature. When he suggests that freedom is prior to truth, he is paying humanity a high compliment; we need not be stuck with *any* so far projected accounts of nonhuman or human reality. Whatever has been so far proposed as an account of what there is or what one ought to do can be changed, corrected, modified, abandoned, or rejected when it proves to be problematic, bothersome, or a blind alley. A close student of the history of Western philosophy, Rorty has found it to be nourished on a one-sided diet[46] and therefore recommends that we try to give freer rein to our imaginations. This is what the talk about edification and hermeneutics in the end comes to.

The observation that in our culture academic professional philosophy has marginalized itself can be interpreted in more than one way.[47] If the discipline has exaggerated ambitions for and expectations from itself, then it will find its peripheral status disappointing. But if we embrace the view of philosophy that Rorty recommends, this conclusion loses its sting. Written with a small "p," the word stands for areas in the culture where the "final vocabulary" is taken with a grain of salt and where it is realized that the pressure of further contingencies may bring about changes in our views. To be alert to such contingencies is to have a looser connection to beliefs and desires now "constituting" our selfhoods and our communities. To say this is, of course, not to suggest that everything in our self-image is up for grabs at once. The stresses and strains are not likely to appear at places where we have sufficient reasons to hold on to our convictions unflinchingly. Only when, as Peirce insisted, we are surprised by the "irritation of a doubt" do we turn honestly to questioning what we so far believed without question.

Seen from this direction, marginalization is not at all deplorable. It is inescapable for anyone who feels the need to step back from the present scene, from conventional wisdom, from truths taken for granted. This holds no more for philosophers than for anyone who needs to sit for a while in an armchair, retreat to brown study, or even escape to the ivory tower. Withdrawal from society may be useful not only for a religious hermit but also for anyone who wishes to do some concentrated thinking. When this need for retreat is taken into account, Rorty's recommendation that the separation of the private from the public be taken seriously looks not only sensible but highly desirable as well. To respect the private realm is to give freedom and hope their greatest scope. When we are told by Rorty that some of Galileo's or Newton's insights might have been caused by a cosmic ray, instead of being an insult to human rationality, this remark may be an acknowledgment that the resources (or potential causes) of intelligence are indeed vaster than we are prepared to admit.[48] Of course, a Newton or an Einstein is *prepared* to react in a fruitful way to a cosmic ray's impact; their background beliefs, practices, and skills had to be of a certain kind for a contingent occurrence to secure an uptake. Most other brains would find even a bombardment by fortuitous "insight-generators" completely meaningless. Nevertheless, the accidental and contingent sources of change in perceptions and beliefs often make all the difference and should be given their due; they should not be ruled out a priori by an "essentialist" theory of mind.

Because in the gray area of our knowledge and understanding one can expect a good deal of blind groping, guessing, experimenting, trying and erring, it is not helpful to be impatient with those who wander off into an uncharted territory. Philosophers are tempted to dispose quickly and definitively of those questions that confuse everyone. Impatient for results, they look for quick certainty. The willingness to acquiesce in such "hard truths" is in part caused by taking the sage and the wise for being wiser and more sagacious than they really are. Importuned by wisdom seekers, philosophers may succumb to the human frailty of appearing, self-deceivingly, as revealers of the Truth and the Secret. The ubiquity of this temptation struck Socrates when he noted that people tend to think that they know when in fact they don't. That's why he thought that his wisdom consisted in knowing that he didn't know.

Rorty's antiepistemological and antimetaphysical stance is an extension of Socratic wisdom. He doesn't think it helpful to look for words that would act like thunderclaps;[49] we can always ask, "What did the thunder say?" Nor does he think that logocentrism or the metaphysics of presence should be replaced by something equally imposing, such as the *absence* of presence. He thinks that Derrida leads us on the primrose path when he says that *différance* is not a concept, and he urges us to be suspicious of thinkers who say that something does not exist.[50] In short, his general strategy is pragmatic: Don't try to be deep; stay on the surface; and ask what real difference to the rest of our language and our practices would the introduction of a term or a theory make. The question does not require an account in terms of vocabulary already in place and governed by established criteria. A new locution or a metaphor does not carry its meaning on its face. To be useful, the new term must eventually enter into the working language; to count as a live metaphor, it must be potentially *dead,* eventually achieving a literal use. That's why a version of the principle of charity can be invoked to allow new terms to *find* a place in language. But the condition of finding it is its possibility of establishing conceptual connections with already existing terms, and this cannot happen if the term in question is said to connect directly with reality or with Being. As such, it is precluded from entering into a framework of linguistic justification, and instead is treated as requiring a special medium of access: intuition, "knowledge by acquaintance," or revelation.

Rorty's campaign against metaphysics, which includes criticism of those who in spite of rejecting it nevertheless managed to fall right back into it (Nietzsche, Heidegger, Derrida), can be seen as but the other side of his wish to avoid what Peirce called "blocking the road to inquiry." But he goes beyond Peirce by suggesting that what he calls "conversation" should not *degenerate* into inquiry,[51] indicating thereby that "inquiry" is more at home in "normal" discourse, where things are settled by appeal to criteria. In contrast, conversation includes revolutionary ventures, where we struggle with anomalies and with other situations with which we don't know how to cope. Here the appeal to criteria or truth will not help us, but neither will the attempt to escape the stubborn particularity of a difficulty by postulating metaphysical realms accessible by a special vocabulary, incommensurate with the rest of language.

A "conversation" with our philosophical ancestors may sometimes require of us to *learn* how they used their vocabularies. A similar effort may be needed when we try to understand contemporary but distant peoples or cultures. Not anxious to pour all humanity into one single mold, discovered by universal metaphysics, we are likely to pay attention to differences among groups of people who grew up in different geographical and historical settings. One consequence of taking a more relaxed attitude toward "overarching truths" would be a greater respect for modes of life that came into existence under circumstances different from ours and were nourished by different sets of metaphors, rituals, and practices. The slogan of the Polish Solidarity movement "Let Poland be Poland!" has application elsewhere.

Leaning on a metaphysical expression introduced by Gadamer, one may be inclined to say that when peoples or social groups affect one another, there may occur a "fusion of horizons." This locution does help us get away from the metaphor of *depth,* favored by a "foundational" mode of thinking about human possibilities. That metaphor has a counterpart in the theological idea of reaching *heights* available to those who respond to the pull of grace from above. Both "depth" and "heights" are "vertical" metaphors. In contrast, Gadamer's talk of "horizons" is clearly "horizontal." When Rorty suggests that in our relations to other human beings we ought to aim at something he calls "solidarity," he is trying to get away from *both* spatial metaphors, "vertical" and "horizontal." Solidarity seems like a good value to aim at, because it brings us back into "human space," the context of relations among beings who have good reasons to think that there may be other things they could share besides those which they already hold in common. True, the increment of sharing is most of the time gradual and almost imperceptible; only after an interval of years or decades do we come to marvel at the fact that we have really changed. (What do the Southerners of today think of who they were in the 1960s?) The invitation toward greater humanization can be discerned also in Rorty's recommendation that we think of choosing our models and canons in terms of choosing our friends and heroes. This recommendation brings on the fact that we try to make our beliefs and desires cohere with one another, and that often we welcome the possibility of making them cohere with the beliefs and the desires of others. That's where the "solidarity" talk comes in.

That term can also be appropriately invoked in contexts where individuals find themselves already "identified" with their communities, in terms of shared ethnic, national, or religious values. In such contexts people can feel united not because the beliefs and commitments they hold in common are an expression of some deeper truth about the essence of humanity as such, expressed in the doctrine of human nature or natural rights, but because they can tell each other stories about their past as an enduring historical community in which some significant communal events occurred. Narratives about such events will mention some outstanding individuals, some exploits in which loyalty, sacrifice, heroism, devotion, persistence, intelligence, and imagination were impressively displayed. The possibility of pointing to a past and present commitment to some traditions, rituals, and institutions provides sufficient reason for celebration and pride, without thereby throwing any aspersions on alternative forms of life manifested by other human groups. The fact that partiality for one's own may at times be expressed by contrasting it with some other traditions can also serve as a reminder that alternative patterns of culture are not found, not already stored up in the genes or in the species, but are made and remade by fluid choices of succeeding generations.

In spite of the fact that the world is becoming a global "village," with news and people traveling ever faster in all directions, it is neither likely nor desirable for humanity to become wholly homogenized. As more and more contacts and mutually interrelated enterprises proliferate, thus creating a need to bring into existence a "common space" among them, not all differences will, or should, be eliminated or overcome. For all viable traits and characteristics adopted by cultures or peoples in the course of their development have survived the test of time at least up to a point, and prevalent customs promise to continue. People are attached to their customs and rituals not only because they provide a social glue, a sense of community; they may also be seen as still unfinished experiments, with more life in them than anyone realizes. So it is not just nostalgia that keeps people attached to their own; there is a hope that the old forms can generate new and welcome variations. The reluctance to let go of one's past and one's tradition is therefore a justifiable confidence in the viability of accumulated wisdom and values.

Nevertheless, openness to other cultures, to other ways of handling practical problems or organizing intellectual activity, is also likely to facilitate change in desirable directions. Here Rorty's emphasis on the edifying and reactive side of thought can have practical consequences. Contact with other cultures and traditions may supply materials in terms of which one's own culture and tradition are likely to be reviewed and reimagined. Just as "normal science" provides the background for revolutionary moves, so received beliefs and practices furnish a backdrop against which foreign ways may be seen. The result of such a comparison may be something new and fresh, marrying a part of the old with parts of the new. Contact between societies may lead to trade-offs and to partial, mutual adjustment. One changes in some respects in order to remain faithful in others. On a large scale this happens when the older cultures of Asia or Africa face the so-called problem of modernization, of blending Western technology with their forms of life. This may become especially acute where religion has been a prominent shaper of daily practices, as is the case in many Islamic and Hindu communities. On the individual level, every person affected by the crossroads of practices and ideas may feel the need to modify the customary style of thinking and behaving.

The question of power naturally arises in such contexts of active interface. Understandably, there is always a fear or suspicion that those wielding greater economic or political power will try to convert "them" into "us," or at least exert pressure to bring about conformity. The negative connotation of "colonization" enshrines this regrettable tendency, sometimes attributed to an innate aggressiveness of the species. But if colonization is repudiated, other forms of domination seem to be still around. As the various "liberation movements" amply demonstrate, the mechanism of domination may be subtle and insidious; those who dominate are seduced to think of themselves as innocent or virtuous.

Global theories, such as Marxism and other ideology-dominated conceptions of the future, strain toward some overarching schemes that would streamline variegated tensions among groups, economically, ethnically, or religiously classified. Oblivious to particularities, they would like to take care of all the conflicts and differences all at once. Dreaming universalist dreams is not limited to Marxists. This perennial ambition of philosophy, attenuated as it may be, still animates such schemes as Habermas's "theory of communicative action." Standing on Dewey's shoulders, Rorty points out that that road, traveled doggedly but unsuccessfully in the past, should be abandoned. A general philosophical solution to the problems of human diversity is not worth trying for—it causes too much pain and injustice. The problems of diversity are practical, pragmatic, and must be addressed in detail. Starting from where we are, from where the shoe pinches or where a promising vista opens up, we are more likely to enter into a fruitful dialogue in which the us-them relationship is shaped by the way the contending parties work toward unforced agreements by persuasion and goodwill. There is no royal road to harmony. There are only multiple paths of mutual accommodation.

Thinking along these lines, we are likely to revise the notion of relativism. Its pejorative connotation dissolves once the idea of one single system of descriptions, evaluations, and interpretations is seen through as a red herring or impostor. There are positive equivalents to the term "relativism." One of them is "diversity," another "pluralism," and still another is "perspectivism." When coupled with Rorty's "solidarity," they form intelligible and defensible conceptual blends. None of these alternatives has a built-in connotation that different cultures or systems of thought *have* to be ranked hierarchically, that there must be a pecking order among them. What Rorty's work has done is to help us discard this relic of the past, an heir to the authoritarian way of thinking—about God, nations, or societies. Authoritarian orders tend to worship quantity, power, machismo. As we know from history, those commanding a larger quantity of material resources are hardly ever greater in a moral sense. The untold sufferings of our century stem directly from attempts of larger nations to interpret the term "great power" as a license for aggressive ventures.

History shows that it is always tempting for those who control all the resources of their people to present their cause—to themselves and to those against whom they proceed—as sanctioned by reality itself, as represented by God or History or Destiny or Nature. They see a link between Truth Itself and their particular cause—the *Gott-mit-uns* syndrome. So if people are dissuaded from viewing their particular causes as based on some eternal or absolute truths about reality or humanity, they are less likely to be vulnerable to mobilization for aggressive stances toward others by those who claim to speak in the name of reality or humanity. An intermediate step in that direction would be to take less seriously an enterprise that sets its sights at providing foundations for all possible truths and essential natures. When spelled with a capital "P," Philosophy feeds the illusion that such an enterprise is possible. By encouraging us to think of philosophy with a small "p," Rorty promotes the idea that humanity is more likely to avoid holocausts and to prosper when philosophy spreads itself around to serve as a commentary, a catalyst, an edifying partner in any intellectual enterprise that serves particular human needs.

This is not a matter of lowering one's sights. Rather, it is on the one hand an invitation to "privatize" philosophy in order to stress its importance for individuals in their personal attempts to make sense of their lives, and on the other hand, in case at some points philosophical reflection of the utopian sort should provide insights and vocabularies useful in the public arena, to make its voice audible in the free market of ideas. That market is likely to be more lively and more productive when the lines between the genres are blurred, when a writer is not kept from exploring his or her ideas fearlessly and fully by the consciousness of conventional limits which the genre imposes. Philosophers will not be afraid to be literary, and novelists will not feel sheepish when in their work they come to express philosophical ideas. The same "freedom of intellectual seas" will be extended to people working in any other sphere of human thought. While traveling in different ships, they will be allowed to discharge and to take on people and cargo in any port.

When Rorty speaks of philosophical activity as aiming at producing delight or *jouissance,* he is reminding us of something that pervades Platonic dialogues and can be found in many other philosophical writings, those of Boethius, Spinoza, or Santayana. That something is hard to pin down but has to do with the exhilarating mood or spirit which unencumbered adventure among ideas sometimes generates. Aristotle tried to capture it in his account of contemplation, ranking intellectual virtues higher than the moral ones. By saying that God's activity consists in thinking about thinking, he paid philosophy the highest compliment. This is the context, I believe, in which we should place Rorty's urging that the private function of philosophy should be given priority over the eventual public applications. For it is in such private good that the actual content and substance of human life resides and where every person should be granted the freedom to fashion that life in the way he or she desires. It can help us become more tolerant, more understanding, and more curious about each other, thereby making the world we live in more humane.

Teaching Philosophy

A plausible answer to the question "What is philosophy?" would be that it is its own history. At least, it would be a good *beginning* to an answer. In a straightforward sense, philosophy is what philosophers have made it. Thus, a natural way to be introduced to the subject is to read the works of thinkers who in the course of time have been accepted as its founders. This is why courses in the history of philosophy usually play a fundamental role in the education of undergraduate majors in philosophy and are often regarded as providing a useful survey of general formative ideas underlying other disciplines as well.

An important result of Rorty's questioning the central role played by epistemology in the Plato-Descartes-Kant tradition is a realization that there are *alternatives* to the critical approach that the tradition favored. Its dogged quest for certainty *called* for criteria, preferably of a universal, ahistorical sort. A succession of theorists tried to outdo each other in producing accounts that would stand the test of time and provide a basis for all future thought—with Plato's Theory of Forms setting the stage, thus encouraging an unending series of "footnotes." Even when they tried to reverse the original texts, successive theorists saw themselves as rivals in the same enterprise: to discover the essence of things.

If the history of philosophy is taught in full realization that it constitutes no more than a series of *experiments* in thought, often ingenious and illuminating, calling attention to aspects of the world either overlooked or slighted by predecessors, if it is seen as a creative enterprise seeking new metaphors and new comparisons, students will cease looking at it as failed attempts to be scientific, to nail things down once and for all. To be sure, the introduction of a new idea, if felicitous, will take time to be explored, ratified, and developed. In some cases it may require several generations of thinkers to lend a sense of continuity to a philosophical process. Not all implications or internal tensions can be explored at once, and it sometimes takes the hard work of brilliant minds either to see through the incoherence in an original idea or theory or to exploit its further possibilities by embroidering upon it in unexpected ways. The histories of the famous three Continental Rationalists—Descartes, Spinoza, and Leibniz—and three British Empiricists—Locke, Berkeley, and Hume—are good examples of such a development.

It is doubtful whether our Western culture would be better off if it followed Hume's advice to consign to flames all books containing theological or metaphysical speculations. While they fail in respects intended by their creators, many metaphysical ventures have succeeded in other ways. As documents in the history of philosophy, they can be read with profit as experiments in thought, the result of which may be a growth in self-understanding on the part of the reader. They may also suggest further thoughts and experiments, some of which may affect some aspects of the public scene. That influence may not always be salutary, especially when the original idea is skewed by commentators and editors in dubious or pernicious directions, as Nietzsche's writings were abused by his sister and by some of his interpreters. Or a thinker may have political ambitions for the application of his views without being sure just how the application will work. Heidegger's case seems to fall in this category. He may have hoped to provide philosophical underpinnings for the National Socialist movement in Germany, but seeing the actual direction of that movement, he stopped looking in his work for political implications and instead concentrated on other dimensions of his thought. These dimensions are original and insightful enough to be of possible use in the private quest for self-perfection, precisely because they swing free of social and political matters.

What is true of the history of philosophy is also true of such subdisciplines as ethics, aesthetics, political theory, or philosophy of science. They all can benefit from explorations analogous to Thomas Kuhn's *The Structure of Scientific Revolutions*. As he showed that science is not a one-dimensional, unilinear progression of theoretical implications smoothly flowing from one into another but is "structured" by the introduction of new paradigms and new ways of inquiry, so it is likely that the changes in the theories of what is good, true, or beautiful are a function of proliferating insights and intuitions which sometimes revolutionized our thinking about these different areas of human experience. The history of such transitions will again be a lesson in creative experimentation in which the images of a good, just, well-ordered society are brought about by the corresponding self-images of people who mustered enough linguistic imagination to manipulate and modify existing descriptions.[52]

The lesson derived from studying philosophy and its subdisciplines in this historicist way will be the realization that our *present* views on what the world is like and what we want our societies to be are amenable to changes, corrections, and departures that are not the result of finding but of making. That making is of course no willful and arbitrary process but has at its disposal the funded wisdom of conclusions that commanded the attention and acceptance of previous generations and is conditioned by the present-day unforced consensus of those who use their best judgment to sort things out in an optimal way. To be rational is to be guided by the best possible opinions generated by people whose competence in the area of interest to us we have good reasons to trust. In this sense, our expertise is an extension of that of others. We are judged and judge ourselves by the authorities we choose. This applies to philosophies we make our own. In urging us to balance the constructive side of theorizing with a reactive one, Rorty is taking into account the importance of *discontinuities* in our efforts to cope. In doing so, he is following the pragmatists' observation that thinking does not really get under way until we are thrown into a "problematic situation" (Dewey) or are suffering the "irritation of a doubt" (Peirce). The eagerness to arrive at certainty predisposes us to favor continuity and to close gaps either by metaphysical constructions (such as "minds" or "mental states") or by wishful thinking (such as "the unified theory of science" or "natural rights"), not surprisingly generating a nagging suspicion that the two modes of manufacturing continuity and universality are really the same.[53] The teaching of philosophy should encourage the thought that what we call critical thinking includes a distrust of continuities and a corresponding openness to alternatives so far uninvented. When Whitehead's motto "Seek simplicity and distrust it" is amended by substituting "continuity" for "simplicity," the student will be encouraged not to "collaborate" with the text too soon, to use the principle of charity only when it is called for, and to be on the lookout for the possibilities of moving in the direction of creative discontinuity. This would make philosophy more fun to teach and to learn.

One reason to encourage the view that philosophy includes a strong interpretive, hermeneutic component is to discourage any form of "philosophical imperialism" or any institutionalized practice that stultifies fresh endeavors and blocks the road to further conversation. This concern has increasingly surfaced in philosophical academic circles.

Critics of the alleged domination of the philosophical profession by analytic philosophers believe that much philosophical talent is being kept from reaching the ranks of the profession. Thus, Charles Sherover claims in an interview in the *New York Times*[54] that "you're much more likely to find philosophically-inclined people outside of philosophy, because if you are philosophically inclined, you've probably been excluded." In this somewhat partisan statement Sherover takes sides with the so-called pluralist movement of professional philosophers, who in recent years decided to "combat what they believe is the control over the field exercised by what they see as a highly technical subspeciality, the Anglo-American analytical school." The pluralist movement has had some success; a number of its representatives were elected to important offices of the American Philosophical Association and have broadened the scope of papers accepted for presentation at annual professional meetings. Although Rorty has not been politically active in this controversy, his views on the nature of philosophy are in harmony with the position taken by the pluralists and thus may have contributed to the fulfillment of their hope to be included in professional conversations and decisions.

One important phenomenon on our cultural scene confirms the soundness of Rorty's view that philosophy should move away from the search for global generalizations to a serious involvement in "local knowledge." The phenomenon I am referring to is "applied philosophy." In recent decades such subspecialties as medical ethics, business ethics, engineering ethics, and agricultural ethics have emerged. Philosophers who have moved into these areas have found that the room for theory is *not reduced* by the practical function that the particular field serves. On the contrary, the marriage of theory and practice enriches both. Although "applied ethics" has its critics, it is unlikely that the professions to which philosophers have attached themselves would be just as happy to dispense with the help they are receiving. It is more likely that this symbiosis will continue. Problems of society are handled better when thoughtful appraisal from many relevant directions is permitted. As Dewey insisted, problems of philosophers are problems of human beings. Just as religion does not necessarily prosper when delivered into the hands of theologians alone, so medicine and law can benefit from those who peek over busy professional shoulders.

An increasingly interdisciplinary conversation is an undisputed fact of our times. Literary theory and social sciences make use of philosophical texts, and philosophers return the compliment. The mutual borrowing may at times be too heavy, making Rorty wonder, for example, whether literary theory wants to take over the role that philosophy is trying to shake off.[55] But on the whole, mutual intellectual stimulation leads to fruitful explorations, rejuvenating the disciplines in question. Rorty's slogan that philosophers should become all-purpose intellectuals could be stated in reverse as well, and it is evident that scholars in the whole spectrum of social and natural sciences often find it necessary to be philosophical.

Another manifestation of the blurring of disciplinary boundaries is the mushrooming of continuing education programs in American universities. More and more people, especially from the older generations, are feeling the appeal of learning, thus giving support to the view that lifelong learning is not such a bad idea. In this form of education, which is becoming increasingly institutionalized (with universities finding more clients to provide services for), people are eager to explore connections that so far have escaped them in their educational and professional careers. Philosophy is among the disciplines benefiting from this phenomenon. A democratized philosophy, spread across the entire field of intellectual endeavor and animated by the sense that whatever we know and believe is touched by the exploratory hand of historical contingency, is likely to provide materials both for "private bliss" and for occasional meditation on the public good. In this arena too the teaching of philosophy can become hopeful.

The Humanism of Pragmatism

One positive consequence of introducing the distinction between Philosophy and philosophy may be a closer attention to the role that ideas play in the culture as a whole. Among Rorty's hopes is that the post-Philosophical culture will be better than the one in which Philosophy insists on ploughing its own furrow. These hopes he expresses as follows:

> This would be a culture in which neither the priests nor the physicists nor the poets nor the Party were thought of as more 'rational,' or more 'scientific' or 'deeper' than one another. No particular portion of culture would be singled out as exemplifying (or signally failing to exemplify) the condition to which the rest aspired. There would be no sense that, beyond the current intradisciplinary criteria, which, for example, good priests or good physicists obeyed, there were other, transdisciplinary, transcultural, ahistorical criteria, which they also obeyed. There would still be hero-worship in such a culture, but it would not be worship of heroes as children of the gods, as marked off from the rest of mankind by closeness to the immortal. It would simply be admiration of exceptional men and women who were very good at doing the quite diverse kinds of things they did. Such people would not be those who knew a Secret, who had won through to the Truth, but simply people who were good at being human.[56]

Rorty acknowledges that such a hypothetical culture would look "decadent" to philosophers like the Platonists and the positivists who want culture "to be *guided,* constrained, not left to its own devices,"[57] and who would not be satisfied with anything less than immortal propositions, rejecting merely mortal vocabularies. As we have seen, such a desire looks to Rorty overly ambitious and in principle unattainable, because ultimately incoherent. Preferring to regard scholarly disciplines as genres of literature, he would afford all of them equal status in the pursuit of what is good in the way of belief. "Physics is a way of trying to cope with various bits of the universe; ethics is a matter of trying to cope with other bits. Mathematics helps physics do its job; literature and the arts help ethics do its."[58] No intellectual enterprise, including philosophy, can produce anything useful if it aims at a sudden discovery of "how things really are," but all of them, in their different ways, can contribute to making a pragmatic sense of the world.

Rorty's is not the only voice that recommends the abandonment of ahistorical approaches in philosophy. His position has been likened to those of Hans-Georg Gadamer and Jürgen Habermas. Comparing the three thinkers, Richard Bernstein finds that they pursue common objectives. All three agree, for instance, that there is no Archimedean point, no theoretical perspective that lies outside our historicity.[59] Of all three Bernstein is prepared to say, employing James's phrase, that the "choice" between foundationalism and non-foundationalism is no longer a "live option."[60] The difference among them is one of emphasis. Gadamer and Habermas still hold out the promise of attaining *knowledge* and *truth,* while Rorty sides with those who would follow Nietzsche in turning their backs on any kind of "metaphysics of presence." Nevertheless, in his article comparing the three thinkers, Bernstein finds "a significant overlap or family resemblance in their respective visions." Concerning Rorty's view, he finds there "a profound moral-political vision that informs his work and suggests what our society may *yet* become."[61] That vision Bernstein likens to James's humanistic pragmatism and cites Rorty's endorsement of its objective to "combine private fulfillment, self-realization, with public morality, a concern for justice."[62] The kind of humanism Rorty has in mind directs us to a "renewed sense of community," repudiated by those who equate community with "disciplinary society" where control is exercised by anonymous powers. "Such a humanism points to the urgency of the practical tasks that confront us in trying to make the world a bit more humane, where our social practices actually become practices whereby we can engage in rational persuasion and *phronesis,* rather than manipulation and strategic maneuvering, and where we seek to root out hidden forms of domination."[63]

Throughout this book I have argued that Rorty finds the reactive, edifying aspect of philosophy to be more important than the constructive, systematic one, because the former preserves the sense of openness, the possibility of ever new values and new discoveries. He criticizes the Platonic tradition in part because he sees in it what Nietzsche called "the will to a system." Such a will, claimed Nietzsche, is a kind of stupidity. What is stupid about it is the presumption that the process of discovery and of creation can come to a full stop, that a particular system of thought can explain and justify everything. Rorty follows Nietzsche in rejecting such a conclusion. In embracing pragmatism he endorses pragmatism's willingness to be the servant of the inexhaustible impulse of life to seek new forms for itself. Plato, the worshipper of the World of Forms, needs to be gotten over. But, as Dewey pointed out, there is also another Plato, the dramatic Plato of Socratic dialogues, who made it clear that not the Forms themselves but their *celebration* is the aim of philosophy.[64] That celebration of course includes knowledge, but it is not exhausted by it. What is important about Forms is that they can also generate love and delight.

So when Rorty recommends delight, he picks up a theme in Plato that has been given only a derivative, secondary status by the tradition that assigns the pride of place to cognition, contemplation, to purely theoretical, mathematized matters. According to John Dewey, the real point of engaging in reconstructive social activities is that they lead to greater human satisfaction, in experiences that are exemplified in the enjoyment of the arts. All of human living, he came to believe, has a consummatory aspect, its end-in-view. This end-in-view is realized in situations in which intelligence liberates us from the routine of habit, thus countering the habit's tendency to reduce the vibrating pulse of life to an inert structure, a frozen form.

Like Dewey, Rorty looks upon playfulness not as confined to mindless frivolities but as lighting up all wakeful, heedful, attentive stretches of life, in which creative human capacities come to the surface. Rorty would agree with Dewey that no appreciation of a work of art can take place when the viewer or listener is not collaborating with the artist by paying attention to what is presented for inspection. Like Dewey, Rorty is willing to generalize from aesthetic experience to ascribe to all areas of life that engage or ought to engage us the capacity to generate their own consummatory enjoyments. Both emphasize the "interestedness" of experience, its living, vibrant character when it is understandingly absorbed, savored, "taken in." Both echo William James's conviction that a pragmatic attitude is not narrowly practical but aims at the satisfaction of the fullest range of interests or "demands."

Rorty favors this side of pragmatism when he directs us toward the reactive and edifying function of thought—the unfamiliar, the abnormal, the revolutionary, the poetic, the metaphorical, the new. There is no danger that their opposites—the familiar, the normal, the prosaic, the literal, the old—will be eliminated or ignored in the process. They are always there as a background for whatever engages our attention. But, as Dewey kept reminding us, when they are allowed to dominate our consciousness, thus routinizing and deadening it, the resulting behavior is converted into what Heidegger attributed to *das Man* in the "inauthentic" mode. To avoid falling into dull averageness and everydayness, we need to keep alive our reactive instincts and impulses. Perhaps it is an exaggeration to say that there are no dull people because there is no dull unconscious, but the paralyzing effect of boredom, ennui, and jadedness are states of mind which not only a Faust would find unbearable. Life resists being swamped by the routine and the familiar, and in that regard pragmatism is squarely on the side of life.

Openness to novelty is an enemy of established criteria and literal meanings. If cognition must have criteria and if openness is the condition of change, then change cannot depend on cognition alone. Those who appreciate this point are sometimes described as romantics. But romanticism may be just another name for creativity. Jacques Barzun claimed that a living civilization oscillates between classic and romantic phases.[65] In this sense, it is quite fitting for Rorty to call himself a romantic, and his philosophical views can be seen as a reaction to the classical Plato-Kant tradition.

If in venturing into novelty one is not "living up" to a preexistent model, not obeying a set of criteria, not expressing an essence, then it may be more appropriate to speak here not of the display of courage to *be* but rather of courage to *act. Am Anfang war die Tat.* "In the beginning was the act." One acts because one does not know what one *is* in such circumstances. And for that one needs courage, a virtue much in demand in a no-man's-land, where there are no signposts. Hans Castorp (in Thomas Mann's *Magic Mountain*) is lost in the snow, a victim of circumstances he cannot control, and yet he is saved by what Mann calls "recklessness." Mann imbues this episode with something *rätselhaft,* mysterious, as if Castorp were tapping some original, instinctive powers of his being. Castorp's "recklessness" could lead to sheer panic, paralyzing fear. But it could also give him a sense of exhilaration, of emboldening hope. The first reaction could induce a Schopenhauerian gloom, and the second a Nietzschean sense of challenge. The first is moved by the principle of fear, the second by the principle of hope. It is significant that from that heightened mingling of recklessness, panic, and danger with hope Castorp achieves, in Mann's telling of the story, an understanding of the meaning of love.

Attentiveness to the leading edge, to the *élan* of life, cannot do without hope. But what is being hoped for is not just novelty, differentness, unfamiliarity. These features of experience emerge against the background of values deposited in memory, the funded knowledge of our traditions. That memory and that knowledge can also furnish warnings against the kind of novelty that may prove dangerous or evil. To be sure, such warnings may sometimes come too late. Every adventure has its risks and may expose us to harm. Past experience cannot guarantee that danger and harm can be avoided. Where there are no clear guidelines, no proven recipes, no final blueprints, there must be hope—if we are to go on living, solving problems, reacting to unforeseen situations. Rorty's humanistic pragmatism is moved by the hope that humanity can keep bringing into being values that will help us cope with life intelligently and effectively.

NOTES

Preface

1. Calvino Romano, in *Voice Literary Supplement, Village Voice,* no. 56 (June 1987): 14–18.

Chapter One: What Can I Know?

1. Richard Rorty, *Philosophy and the Mirror of Nature,* p. 167.

2. Ibid., p. 144.

3. Ibid., p. 183.

4. Ibid., p. 161.

5. Richard Rorty, *Consequences of Pragmatism,* p. 154.

6. Richard Rorty, "Pragmatism, Categories, and Language," p. 219.

7. Rorty, *Philosophy and the Mirror of Nature,* pp. 180–86.

8. J. L. Austin's comments on the use of the adjective "real" as essentially negative also helped drive some nails into the coffin of the distinction between appearance and reality (although it is well to remember Dewey's observation that the proper opposite of appearance is not reality but *dis*appearance). See J. L. Austin, *Sense and Sensibilia,* p. 70.

9. Rorty, *Philosophy and the Mirror of Nature,* p. 276.

10. Ibid., p. 84.

11. "How do I know that this color is red?—It would be an answer to say: 'I've learnt English'" (Ludwig Wittgenstein, *Philosophical Investigations,* #381). This often-quoted remark has thought-provoking antecedents. When Wittgenstein says (#16) that it causes least confusion to regard samples as part of the language of colors, he is undercutting the temptation to create a gap between language and the world. If Wittgenstein's almost casually dropped recommendation is taken seriously, the so-called "problem of the external world," plaguing almost the entire sweep of Western epistemology, would never have arisen. Arguments for this conclusion are presented in my paper "Avoiding the Fly-bottle," at the Wittgenstein Symposium in Kirchberg, Austria, in August 1989.

12. Rorty, "Pragmatism, Categories, and Language."

13.   Richard Rorty, *Contingency, Irony, and Solidarity,* pp. 5–6.

14.   Ibid., p. 5.

15.   Rorty, *Consequences of Pragmatism,* p. 15.

16.   According to Henry LeRoy Finch, the world for Wittgenstein is an expressive phenomenon, and objectivity involves the acceptance of appearances. Finch describes this outlook as "physiognomical" (*Wittgenstein—the Later Philosophy,* p. 190). Finch also warns that "the *Faced World* cannot be talked about without being turned into the *World Said,*" and that "it includes also the *content* of the world, or the sheer qualitative immediacy" (p. 244).

17.   Cf. a general remark by Wittgenstein: "If you are not certain of any fact, you cannot be certain of the meaning of your words either" (*On Certainty,* ¶114).

18.   Rorty, *Consequences of Pragmatism,* p. 195.

19.   Rorty, *Philosophy and the Mirror of Nature,* p. 174.

20.   Ibid., p. 176.

21.   Rorty recommends that we "limit the opposition between rational and irrational forms of persuasion to the interior of a language game," but not "try to apply it to interesting and important shifts in linguistic behavior" (*Contingency, Irony, and Solidarity,* p. 47).

22.   Ibid., p. 18.

23.   Ibid., p. 22.

24.   Ibid., p. 10.

25.   Donald Davidson, "A Nice Derangement of Epitaphs," p. 174.

26.   Rorty, *Contingency, Irony, and Solidarity,* p. 14.

27.   Ibid., p. 16.

28.   Ibid.

29.   Ibid., p. 20.

30.   Ibid., p. 11.

31.   In his book *Nothing Is Hidden,* Norman Malcolm brings out forcefully this consequence of Wittgenstein's philosophy.

32.   Rorty, *Contingency, Irony, and Solidarity,* p. 27.

33.   Ibid., p. 35.

34.   Ibid.

35.   Cf. Alexander Nehamas, *Nietzsche: Life as Literature,* pp. 232–33: "Nietzsche's texts therefore do not describe but, in exquisitely elaborate detail, *exemplify* the perfect instance of his ideal character. And this charac-

ter is none other than the character these very texts constitute: Nietzsche himself."

36. Rorty, *Contingency, Irony, and Solidarity,* p. 33.

37. Ibid., p. 37.

38. John Dewey, *Art as Experience,* p. 53.

39. Rorty, *Contingency, Irony, and Solidarity,* p. 42.

40. Ibid., p. 57.

41. Ibid., p. 45.

42. Ibid., p. 54.

43. Ibid., p. 60.

44. Ibid., p. 58.

45. Immanuel Kant, *Critique of Pure Reason,* A805 = B833.

46. Marcus G. Singer, *Generalization in Ethics,* chap. 8.

47. I have argued this point in my article "Professor Ebbinghaus' Interpretation of the Categorical Imperative": "In conclusion, I would like to suggest that the categorical imperative is an important principle because it gives expression to our awareness of others and to our concern for their moral ends. It is important because men have certain moral concerns, such as truth-telling, helpfulness, mutual trust, cooperation. In the absense of such concerns the categorical imperative would have no application because there would be nothing to which it ought to be applied. But *where* it ought to be applied is a question of moral knowledge which the categorical imperative, of itself, cannot supply" (p. 77).

48. According to Kant, "Every interest is ultimately practical, even that of speculative reason being only conditional and reaching perfection only in practical use" (*Critique of Practical Reason,* p. 126).

49. Kant, *Critique of Pure Reason,* A814 = B842.

50. "Everything in nature works according to laws. Only a rational being has the capacity of acting according to the conception of laws, i.e., according to principles" (Immanuel Kant, *Foundations of the Metaphysics of Morals,* p. 29).

51. William James, *The Writings of William James,* p. 380.

52. Ibid., p. 381.

53. "Words have their meaning only in the flow of life" (Ludwig Wittgenstein, *Last Writings on the Philosophy of Psychology,* 1:118). According to Norman Malcolm, Wittgenstein's claim that "words and sentences can be understood only in terms of the circumstances, the contexts, the life-surroundings, in which they are spoken" deserves special emphasis. He

adds, however, that "this is a teaching that has not, for the most part, been taken in by present-day philosophy" (*Nothing Is Hidden,* p. 239).

54. "To a partly novel situation the response itself is necessarily partly novel, else it is not a response" (Gilbert Ryle, "Improvisation," p. 73).

55. "To use an objectionable phrase, there is nothing 'mental' about sensations" (Gilbert Ryle, *The Concept of Mind,* p. 204).

56. Rorty, *Contingency, Irony, and Solidarity,* p. 34.

57. "All human beings carry about a set of words which they employ to justify their actions, their beliefs, and their lives. These are the words in which we formulate praise of our friends and contempt for our enemies, our long-term projects, our deepest self-doubts and our highest hopes. They are the words in which we tell, sometimes prospectively and sometimes retrospectively, the story of our lives. I shall call these words a person's 'final vocabulary'" (Rorty, *Contingency, Irony, and Solidarity,* p. 73).

58. John Dewey, *Human Nature and Conduct,* p. 196.

59. Rorty's doubts that epistemology, seen as a master philosophical project, can discover Nature's Own Language are paralleled and reinforced by misgivings voiced in the posthumously published diaries of the Polish writer Witold Gombrowicz, who also looks askance at the imperialist tendencies of analytical reason: "I can't believe that Socrates, Spinoza, or Kant were real people and completely serious ones at that. I claim that an excess of seriousness is conditioned by an excess of frivolity. Of what were these majestic conceptions born? Curiosity? Accident? Ambition? Gain? For pleasure? We will never know the dirt of their genesis, their hidden, intimate immaturity, their childhood or shame because even the artists themselves are not allowed to know about this. We will not know the roads by which Kant-the-child and Kant-the-adolescent changed into Kant-the-philosopher, but it would be good to remember that culture or knowledge is something much lighter than one would imagine. Lighter and more ambivalent. Nevertheless, the imperialism of reason is horrible. Whenever reason notices that some part of reality eludes it, it immediately lunges at it to devour it" (*Diary,* pp. 184–85).

Chapter Two: What Ought I to Do?

1. Rorty, *Consequences of Pragmatism,* p. xxxix.

2. Rorty, *Contingency, Irony, and Solidarity,* p. 35.

3. Ibid., p. 32.

4. Ibid., p. 30.

5. Ibid., p. 32.

6. Ibid., p. 36.

7. Ibid., p. 37.

8. William James, "On a Certain Blindness in Human Beings," p. 143.

9. Rorty, *Contingency, Irony, and Solidarity,* p. 35.

10. "The real advantage which truth has consists in this, that when an opinion is true, it may be extinguished once, twice, or many times, but in the course of ages there will generally be found persons to rediscover it, until some one of its reappearances falls on a time when from favorable circumstances it escapes persecution until it has made such head as to withstand all subsequent attempts to suppress it" (John Stuart Mill, *On Liberty,* in *The English Philosophers from Bacon to Mill,* p. 971).

11. Rorty, *Contingency, Irony, and Solidarity,* chap. 8.

12. Ibid., p. 178.

13. Ibid., p. 34.

14. Ibid., p. 37.

15. Ibid., p. 46.

16. Ibid., p. 33.

17. Cf. David L. Norton's analysis of *daimon* in his *Personal Destinies,* p. 5, and also an articulation of the notion of personhood in my *Cosmic Religion: An Autobiography of the Universe,* pp. 23–66.

18. Richard Rorty, "Priority of Democracy to Philosophy," p. 257.

19. Michael Sandel, *Liberalism and the Limits of Justification,* p. 19.

20. Rorty, "Priority of Democracy to Philosophy," p. 259.

21. Ibid., p. 261.

22. Ibid., p. 263.

23. Ibid., p. 263.

24. Rorty, *Contingency, Irony, and Solidarity,* p. 46.

25. Rorty, "Priority of Democracy to Philosophy," p. 268.

26. Ibid., p. 272.

27. A society free from domination is tellingly characterized by Michael Walzer: "No more bowing and scraping, fawning and toadying; no more fearful trembling; no more high-and-mightiness; no more masters, no more slaves" (*Spheres of Justice,* p. xiii).

28. Rorty, "Priority of Democracy to Philosophy," p. 269.

29. Rorty, "Posties," p. 11.

30. Ibid., p. 12.

31. Ibid., p. 274.

32. Rorty, *Philosophy and the Mirror of Nature,* pp. 320–21.

33. This is the theme of my book, *The Freedom of Reason.*

34. Rorty, *Consequences of Pragmatism,* pp. 51, 203.

35. Ibid., p. 100.

36. Rorty notes Judith Shklar's criterion of a liberal: "Somebody who believes that cruelty is the worst thing we do" (*Contingency, Irony, and Solidarity,* p. 146).

37. Ibid., p. 157ff.

38. Fyodor Dostoyevsky, *Notes from Underground,* p. 36.

39. George Santayana, "Ultimate Religion," pp. 292–93.

40. Joseph Conrad, *Heart of Darkness,* p. 112.

Chapter Three: What May I Hope?

1. "The rational meaning of every proposition lies in the future. How so? The meaning of a proposition is itself a proposition." Charles Sanders Peirce, *Collected Papers,* 5.427.

2. Peirce, *Collected Papers,* 2.330.

3. Rorty, *Consequences of Pragmatism,* p. 208.

4. Ibid., p. 203.

5. Ibid., p. 47.

6. Ibid., p. 202.

7. The phenomena described here I tried to subsume under the notion of "participation": "Our ordinary perceptions already include an element of sharedness and participation. We participate in the experiences of others by characterizing and describing our common world" (*Religion without God,* p. 45).

8. *Contingency, Irony, and Solidarity,* pp. 48–49.

9. Rorty, *Consequences of Pragmatism,* p. 172.

10. "Davidson lets us think of the history of language, and thus of culture, as Darwin taught us to think of the history of a coral reef" (*Contingency, Irony, and Solidarity,* p. 16).

11. "Why do I always speak of being compelled by a rule, why not of the fact that I can *choose* to follow it? For that is equally important.

"But I don't want to say, either, that the rule compels me to act like this; but that it makes it possible for me to hold by it and make it compel me" (Ludwig Wittgenstein, *Remarks on the Foundations of Mathematics,* p. 193).

12. The failure of our educational institutions to impart even a minimal cultural literacy is causing a great deal of concern. Cf. E. D. Hirsch, *Cultural Literacy.*

13. J. W. Goethe, *Faust,* p. 42.

14. See Konstantin Kolenda, ed., *Organizations and Ethical Individualism.*

15. Rorty, "Priority of Democracy to Philosophy," p. 269.

16. Richard Bernstein, "One Step Forward, Two Steps Backward: Richard Rorty on Liberal Democracy and Philosophy," p. 556.

17. Rorty, "Posties."

18. Richard Rorty, "Thugs and Theorists: A Reply to Bernstein," p. 570.

19. Ibid., p. 567.

20. Mikhail S. Gorbachev, *Toward a Better World,* p. 4.

21. Ibid., p. 4.

22. Ibid., p. 12.

23. Ibid., p. 4.

24. Mikhail S. Gorbachev, *Perestroika,* p. 221.

25. Ibid., p. 224.

26. Ibid., p. 158.

27. In an unpublished paper, "Unger, Castoriadis, and the Romance of a National Future," Rorty suggests that sweeping changes of this sort are not likely to be the result of a philosophical or political theory but of some concrete experiment.

Chapter Four: Hope and Philosophy

1. Richard J. Bernstein, *Philosophical Profiles,* p. 21.

2. Daniel Dennett, "Comments on Rorty," p. 349.

3. C. G. Prado, *The Limits of Pragmatism,* p. 20.

4. Ibid., p. 77.

5. Ibid., p. 88.

6. John Caputo, "The Thought of Being and the Conversation of Mankind: The Case of Heidegger and Rorty."

7. Donald Davidson, "On the Very Idea of a Conceptual Scheme," p. 20.

8. Wittgenstein, *Philosophical Investigations,* ¶290: "To use a word without a justification does not mean to use it without right."

9. Prado, *The Limits of Pragmatism,* p. 108.

10. Ibid., p. 132.

11. Ibid., p. 133. What we make of the world is reflected in the language we use. This Wittgensteinian point is often unaccountably overlooked. Elizabeth H. Wolgast has recently reminded us of its force in her book *The Grammar of Justice.* She tells us that "Wittgenstein admonishes us not only to look at a noun as if it showed us the metaphysical status of what it means. Rather we need to think of the way the word is woven into grammatical patterns—orders, questions, protests, expressions of our states—and these patterns integrated into our lives. When we have seen how it works, understood its grammar, we will have grasped its meaning" (p. 140). As Rorty reminds us, "Nature is whatever is so routine and familiar that we trust our language implicitly" (*Philosophy and the Mirror of Nature,* p. 352).

12. Bernstein, "One Step Forward, Two Steps Backward," pp. 549–50.

13. David R. Hiley, *Philosophy in Question,* p. 111.

14. Ibid., p. 144.

15. John Dewey, *The Philosophy of John Dewey,* 2:647–48.

16. Alasdair MacIntyre, *After Virtue,* chap. 2.

17. John Rawls, *A Theory of Justice,* p. 579.

18. Rorty, "A Reply to Dreyfus and Taylor," p. 39, and Rorty, *Consequences of Pragmatism,* p. 199.

19. Richard J. Bernstein, "Philosophy in the Conversation of Mankind," p. 768. Reprinted in *Hermeneutics and Praxis,* p. 54.

20. John Dunn, *Rethinking Modern Political Theory,* p. 174. Also cf. my "Rorty's Dewey."

21. Cornel West, "The Politics of American Neo-Pragmatism," p. 267.

22. Ibid.

23. Ibid., p. 268.

24. Ibid., p. 269.

25. Ibid., p. 271.

26. John R. Wallach, "Liberals, Communitarians, and the Task of Political Theory," p. 599.

27. Ibid., p. 600. Interestingly enough, Wallach's own account of citizenship seems to parallel the dialectic between normal and abnormal,

systematic and edifying discourse: "Democratic citizens exercising their deliberative powers are at once inside *and* outside their political community" (p. 602, italics in text).

28. Jeffrey Stout, "Liberal Society and the Languages of Morals," p. 45.

29. Ibid., p. 46.

30. Ibid., p. 48.

31. Ibid., p. 50.

32. Ibid., p. 54.

33. Ibid., p. 51.

34. Ibid., p. 56.

35. Hiley, *Philosophy in Question,* p. 165.

36. Charles Guignon, "Saving the Difference: Gadamer and Rorty," p. 361.

37. Hiley, *Philosophy in Question,* p. 163.

38. Herbert Marcuse, *One-Dimensional Man,* p. 11.

39. Hiley, *Philosophy in Question,* p 166.

40. Ibid., p. 163.

41. Ibid., p. 173.

42. Rorty, *Philosophy and the Mirror of Nature,* p. 394.

43. Rorty, *Consequences of Pragmatism,* p. 217.

44. Rorty, *Philosophy and the Mirror of Nature,* p. 365. At the XI Inter-American Congress of Philosophy in Guadalajara, Mexico, Rorty presented a paper which some Latin American and Canadian philosophers perceived as another instance of Euro-American bias. This reaction, I believe, was based on a misunderstanding. In a comment on a correspondence generated by this occasion, I pointed out that Rorty's position "is not inimical to the celebration of cultural differences and of national endeavors to give form, character, a unique style of life within a particular historical context" (Kolenda, "Letters to the Editor," *Proceedings and Addresses of the American Philosophical Association,* vol. 60, no. 1, September 1986, p. 71).

45. Rorty, *Philosophy and the Mirror of Nature,* pp. 370–71.

46. "A main cause of philosophical disease—a one-sided diet: one nourishes one's thinking with only one kind of example" (Ludwig Wittgenstein, *Philosophical Investigations,* ¶593).

47. Rorty, "Postmodernist Bourgeois Liberalism," *Journal of Philosophy,* 80, 1983.

48. Doubtful that it is possible to develop a general theory that would ground causal explanations of historical developments in science, Rorty, in a letter to Thomas Kuhn, expressed his doubts as follows: "I should have thought that such getting such explanations was a matter of spinning convincing narratives which bring together all kinds of causes: somebody's having developed a new technique for grinding lenses, the anti-Aristotelian currents running through universities in the 16th century, the ability of various secular rulers to resist papal pressure, the particular location of some heavenly bodies when Galileo happened to get a cloudless night, the Rise of the Bourgeoisie, the needs of the navigators, dim memories of Buridan, some particularly neat metaphors which came to Galileo after a particularly good meal, various Platonic-mathematico-Augustinian sorts of mystical theology which had made headway in Italy after Ficino, the verve of publicists like Hobbes, and so on."

49. "The ultimate business of philosophy is to preserve the *force of the most elemental words* in which Dasein expresses itself, and to keep the common understanding from levelling them off to that unintelligibility which functions in turn as a source of pseudo-problems" (Martin Heidegger, *Being and Time,* p. 262).

50. Regarding Derrida's claim that "the trace itself does not exist," Rorty remarks: "One can comment cynically on this passage that, if you want to know what notion takes the place of God for a writer in the onto-theological tradition, always look for one which he says does not exist" (*Consequences of Pragmatism,* p. 102).

51. Rorty, *Philosophy and the Mirror of Nature,* p. 372.

52. According to Lisa Portmess, Rorty's view of philosophy would encourage teaching that would stress the changing cultural and historical character of philosophical problems ("An Historicist View of Teaching Philosophy").

53. "Where our language suggests a body and there is none: there we should like to say, is a *spirit*" (Wittgenstein, *Philosophical Investigations,* ¶36).

54. *New York Times,* 29 December 1987, p. 1.

55. In his presentation at the NEH Institute on Interpretation at the University of California at Santa Cruz in July 1988, Rorty attributed this desire to literary critics Paul de Man and J. Hillis Miller.

56. Rorty, *Consequences of Pragmatism,* pp. xxxviii-xxxix.

57. Ibid., p. xxxix.

58. Ibid., p. xliii.

59. Bernstein, *Philosophical Profiles,* p. 63.

60. Ibid., p. 91.

61. Ibid., p. 87.

62. Rorty, *Consequences of Pragmatism,* p. 158.

63. Bernstein, *Philosophical Profiles,* p. 93.

64. "Nothing could be more helpful to present philosophizing than a 'Back-to-Plato' movement; but it would have to be back to the dramatic, restless, co-operatively inquiring Plato of the Dialogues, trying one mode of attack after another to see what it might yield; back to the Plato whose highest flight of metaphysics always terminated with a social and practical turn, and not to the artificial Plato constructed by unimaginative commentators who treat him as the original university professor" (John Dewey, *On Experience, Nature, and Freedom,* p. 13).

65. Jacques Barzun, *Classic, Romantic, Modern.*

BIBLIOGRAPHY

Austin, J. L. *Sense and Sensibilia.* New York: Oxford University Press, 1964.

Barzun, Jacques. *Classic, Romantic, Modern.* Boston: Little, Brown, 1961.

Bernstein, Richard J. "One Step Forward, Two Steps Backward: Richard Rorty on Liberal Democracy and Philosophy." *Political Theory,* vol. 15, no. 4 (1987):538–63.

———. *Philosophical Profiles.* Philadelphia: University of Pennsylvania Press, 1986.

———. "Philosophy in the Conversation of Mankind." *Review of Metaphysics* (1980): 745–75. Reprinted in *Hermeneutics and Praxis,* edited by Robert Hollinger, 54–86. Notre Dame, Ind.: University of Notre Dame Press, 1985.

Caputo, John. "The Thought of Being and the Conversation of Mankind: The Case of Heidegger and Rorty." *Review of Metaphysics* 36 (1983): 661–85.

Conrad, Joseph. *Heart of Darkness.* New York: Washington Square Press, 1967.

Davidson, Donald. "A Nice Derangement of Epitaphs." In *Philosophical Grounds of Rationality,* edited by R. E. Grandy and R. Warner. Oxford: Clarendon Press, 1986.

———. "On the Very Idea of a Conceptual Scheme." *Proceedings of the American Philosophical Association* 17 (1973–74): 5–20.

Dennett, Daniel. "Comments on Rorty." *Synthese* 53 (1982): 349.

Dewey, John. *Art as Experience.* New York: Capricorn Books, 1958.

———. *Human Nature and Conduct.* New York: Modern Library, 1930.

———. *On Experience, Nature, and Freedom.* Edited by Richard J. Bernstein. Indianapolis: Bobbs-Merrill, 1960.

————. *The Philosophy of John Dewey.* Edited by John J. McDermott. New York: G. P. Putnam's Sons, 1973.

Dostoyevsky, Fyodor. *Notes from Underground.* Translated by Ralph E. Matlaw. New York: E. P. Dutton, 1960.

Dunn, John. *Rethinking Modern Political Theory.* Cambridge: Cambridge University Press, 1985.

Finch, Henry LeRoy. *Wittgenstein—the Later Philosophy.* Atlantic Highlands, N.J.: Humanities Press, 1972.

Goethe, J. W. *Faust.* Translated by B. Q. Morgan. New York: Liberal Arts Press, 1954.

Gombrowicz, Witold. *Diary.* Vol. 1. Translated by Lillian Vallee. Evanston, Ill.: Northwestern University Press, 1988.

Gorbachev, Mikhail S. *Perestroika.* New York: Harper and Row, 1987.

————. *Toward a Better World.* New York: Richardson & Steirman, 1987.

Guignon, Charles. "Saving the Difference: Gadamer and Rorty." *Philosophy of Science Association* 2 (1982): 360–67.

Heidegger, Martin. *Being and Time.* Translated by John Macquarrie and Edward Robinson. New York: Harper & Row, 1962.

Hiley, David R. *Philosophy in Question.* Chicago: University of Chicago Press, 1988.

Hirsch, E. D. *Cultural Literacy.* Boston: Houghton Mifflin, 1987.

James, William. "On a Certain Blindness in Human Beings." In *Talks to Teachers on Psychology,* edited by Frederick Burkhardt and Fredson Bowers. Cambridge, Mass.: Harvard University Press, 1983.

————. *The Writings of William James.* Edited by John J. McDermott. Chicago: University of Chicago Press, 1977.

Kant, Immanuel. *Critique of Practical Reason.* Translated by Lewis White Beck. New York: Liberal Arts Press, 1956.

————. *Critique of Pure Reason.* Translated by Norman Kemp Smith. London: Macmillan, 1950.

————. *Foundations of the Metaphysics of Morals.* Translated by Lewis White Beck. New York: Liberal Arts Press, 1959.

Kolenda, Konstantin. *Cosmic Religion: An Autobiography of the Universe.* Prospect Heights, Ill.: Waveland Press, 1987.

———. *The Freedom of Reason.* San Antonio: Principia Press of Trinity University, 1964.

———. "Letters to the Editor." *Proceedings and Addresses of the American Philosophical Association,* vol. 60, no. 1 (September 1986): 71–73.

———. "Professor Ebbinghaus' Interpretation of the Categorical Imperative." *Philosophical Quarterly,* vol. 5, no. 18 (January 1955): 74–77.

———. *Religion without God.* Buffalo, N.Y.: Prometheus Books, 1976.

———. "Rorty's Dewey." *Journal of Value Inquiry* 20 (1986): 57–62.

MacIntyre, Alasdair. *After Virtue.* Notre Dame, Ind.: University of Notre Dame Press, 1984.

Malcolm, Norman. *Nothing Is Hidden.* Oxford: Basil Blackwell, 1986.

Marcuse, Herbert. *One-Dimensional Man.* Boston: Beacon Press, 1964.

Mill, John Stuart. *On Liberty.* In *The English Philosophers from Bacon to Mill,* edited by E. A. Burtt. New York: Modern Library, 1939.

Nehamas, Alexander. *Nietzsche: Life as Literature.* Cambridge, Mass.: Harvard University Press, 1985.

Norton, David L. *Personal Destinies.* Princeton, N.J.: Princeton University Press, 1976.

Peirce, Charles Sanders. *Collected Papers.* Cambridge, Mass.: Harvard University Press, 1934.

Portmess, Lisa. "An Historicist View of Teaching Philosophy." *Teaching Philosophy* 7 (1984): 313–23.

Prado, C. G. *The Limits of Pragmatism.* Atlantic Highlands, N.J.: Humanities Press, 1987.

Rawls, John. *A Theory of Justice.* Cambridge, Mass.: Harvard University Press, 1971.

Rorty, Richard. *Consequences of Pragmatism.* Minneapolis: University of Minnesota Press, 1982.

———. *Contingency, Irony, and Solidarity.* Cambridge: Cambridge University Press, 1989.

————. *Philosophy and the Mirror of Nature.* Princeton: Princeton University Press, 1979.

————. "Posties." *London Review of Books* 3 (September 1987): 11–12.

————. "Postmodern Bourgeois Liberalism." *Journal of Philosophy* 80 (1983).

————. "Pragmatism, Categories, and Language." *Philosophical Review* (1961): 197–223.

————. "Priority of Democracy to Philosophy." In *The Virginia Statute for Religious Freedom,* edited by Merrill D. Peterson and Robert C. Vaughan. Cambridge: Cambridge University Press, 1988.

————. "Thugs and Theorists: A Reply to Bernstein." *Political Theory,* vol. 15, no. 4 (1987): 564–80.

————. "Unger, Castoriadis, and the Romance of a National Future." Unpublished.

Ryle, Gilbert. *The Concept of Mind.* New York: Barnes and Noble, 1949.

————. "Improvisation." *Mind,* vol. 85, no. 337 (January 1976): 69–83. Reprinted in *On Thinking.* Oxford: Basil Blackwell, 1979.

Sandel, Michael. *Liberalism and the Limits of Justification.* Cambridge: Cambridge University Press, 1982.

Santayana, George. "Ultimate Religion." In *Obiter Scripta.* New York: Charles Scribner's Sons, 1936.

Singer, Marcus G. *Generalization in Ethics.* New York: A. A. Knopf, 1961.

Stout, Jeffrey. "Liberal Society and the Languages of Morals." *Soundings* (Spring/Summer 1986): 32–59.

Wallach, John R. "Liberals, Communitarians, and the Task of Political Theory." *Political Theory,* vol. 15, no. 4 (November 1987): 581–611.

Walzer, Michael. *Spheres of Justice.* New York: Basic Books, 1983.

West, Cornel. "The Politics of American Neo-Pragmatism." In *Post-Analytic Philosophy,* edited by John Rajchman and Cornel West. New York: Columbia University Press, 1985.

Wittgenstein, Ludwig. *Last Writings on the Philosophy of Psychol-*

ogy. Edited by G. H. von Wright and Heikki Nyman. Oxford: Basil Blackwell, 1982.

————. *On Certainty.* Oxford: Basil Blackwell, 1969.

————. *Philosophical Investigations.* New York: Macmillan, 1953.

————. *Remarks on the Foundations of Mathematics.* Cambridge, Mass.: MIT Press, 1956.

Wolgast, Elizabeth H. *The Grammar of Justice.* Ithaca: Cornell University Press, 1987.

INDEX